CONSENT ON CAMPUS

CONSENT ON CAMPUS

A Manifesto

Donna Freitas

OXFORD
UNIVERSITY PRESS

Oxford University Press is a department of the University of Oxford. It furthers
the University's objective of excellence in research, scholarship, and education
by publishing worldwide. Oxford is a registered trade mark of Oxford University
Press in the UK and certain other countries.

Published in the United States of America by Oxford University Press
198 Madison Avenue, New York, NY 10016, United States of America.

Library of Congress Cataloging-in-Publication Data
Names: Freitas, Donna, author.
Title: Consent on campus : a manifesto / Donna Freitas.
Description: New York, NY : Oxford University Press, [2018] | Includes index.
Identifiers: LCCN 2018001913 (print) | LCCN 2018021393 (ebook) |
ISBN 9780190671167 (updf) | ISBN 9780190671174 (epub) |
ISBN 9780190671150 (hardcover)
Subjects: LCSH: Rape in universities and colleges—United States—Prevention. |
College students—Sexual behavior—United States. | Sexual consent—United States. |
Sexual ethics—United States.
Classification: LCC LB2345.3.R37 (ebook) | LCC LB2345.3.R37 F74 2018 (print) |
DDC 371.7/82—dc23
LC record available at https://lccn.loc.gov/2018001913

9 8 7 6 5 4 3 2 1

Printed by Sheridan Books, Inc., United States of America

CONTENTS

PART III Telling the Story of Consent: Rewriting and Transforming Campus Narratives

PREFACE

DEAR ALL UNIVERSITY PRESIDENTS . . .

When I first thought about writing this book, a manifesto really, about the crisis of sexual assault on campus, someone asked me who the audience would be. I answered, only slightly joking:

"Everyone."

Pressed for a more specific response, I blurted out:

"Every single college president in the United States."

When these words came out of my mouth, so forcefully and passionately, I was surprised. Until that moment I hadn't quite realized that, yes, I wanted every college president in America to read this book. Felt that they needed to read this book.

I wanted to reach the faculty, too—that I'd already known to my core. The faculty are some of the most important and influential people on campus and in many ways are the people best positioned to address the issues at hand. And I wanted to reach the students, of course, because they are at the heart of this crisis. And the Student Affairs people, because they are my people, too; I worked in Residence Life for six years when I was a graduate student. But perhaps the most important audience for this book, however audacious it might sound, is university presidents.

I will tell you why.

I've spent the last decade lecturing all over the United States about my research on sex and hookup culture on campus. The campuses where the president shows up for these conversations— or any conversation with students about anything to do with sex and relationships—have completely different climates than other campuses. The faculty, too—don't get me wrong—are tremendously important to the climate, but there is just something about the president of the college taking the time to show that she or he cares that makes an enormous difference. It empowers everyone to take up the conversation and with gusto.

I'll give you an example—one of the most memorable of the 150 or so lectures I've given about sex on all types of campuses. A Catholic liberal arts college not far from Chicago invited me to give the annual lecture that the college president hosts each year in March. Prior to my visit, the president met with a faculty and staff reading group on a regular basis to discuss my book *Sex and the Soul*. When I arrived on campus, the president hosted a dinner with the reading group and some faculty and staff to welcome me. At one point during the dinner, he smiled, chuckled a bit, and told me:

"You know, there's a rumor going around among the students that I'm very angry you're here."

"Wait—what?" I asked, confused by what he meant, since he was obviously not angry and was about as welcoming and jovial as anyone I've met during a campus visit.

This president is also a member of a Catholic order of brothers, which is an essential piece of this story.

"Well," he went on to explain, "the students think I am against all talk of sex, so they believe that you're here against my wishes." At this point everyone else at the table, the faculty and staff, chuckled along with him.

In that moment, I realized how important it was that the students—and everyone else on campus who might have doubts—know that I was at this university to lecture at the president's invitation.

On the afternoon of my talk, the hall was packed with hundreds of people, mostly students, but many faculty and staff as well. Everyone was mixed in together—all these different members of the community sitting with each other in an effort to think and reflect about sex on campus. Somewhere around the third or fourth row was the president, wearing that same welcoming smile he'd had on his face during dinner. As I stood at the front of the lecture hall, I wondered whether the students even realized he was there. The first thing I did as I welcomed everyone was to point out who was in attendance. I asked students to raise their hands first, then student staff (the resident assistants), then professional staff (Student Affairs and Campus Ministry). Then I asked all the faculty in the room to stand up—and there were many, perhaps the most I've ever had at one of my lectures. I wanted the students to see, to notice, every single member of the faculty in the room, so they would also know that the faculty are people who are willing to come to the table to talk with them about sex on campus—that these faculty were open and willing conversation partners. But the last thing I did was mention the rumors I'd been told regarding the president, and I explained that he was, in fact, sitting there in the audience. Then I asked him to stand up and wave at the large crowd—which he did.

A ripple of whispers moved through the audience.

The students were fairly stunned to see him, I think. In a good way.

His presence mattered a great deal to them. It let new air into the room and allowed people to breathe, to sigh with relief, as they realized the following: The president is here at the table with us for this discussion. The president cares. The president is open. The president wants us to think about this. The president wants to think about this with us—with all of us. He is one among many possible conversation partners in our community, and his presence empowers the rest of us, gives us permission to think about this issue critically and honestly.

Showing up for an hour-long lecture may seem like such a small thing, so insignificant and not even that taxing—the president walked into the hall and sat down in a chair where the students could see him. How much, really, does that cost a president? Nearly nothing. But the impact of this act on the students was tremendous. The same goes for the presence of so many faculty. Just by being there, they told the students that thinking and talking about sex in its many and complicated dimensions was both intellectually worthy and institutionally worthy. It was something they were going to talk about and think about on this campus, and everyone would be involved, both inside the classroom and out.

I wish all campuses were like this. It's not the answer to everything, but it goes a long way toward facilitating conversation around sexual assault and consent. And that is a conversation that needs to happen on every campus if we are going to transform our campuses for the better.

I will give you another example of the effect a college president can have, one that is less admirable, before I move on.

The preface to my first book about college campus life, *Sex and the Soul*, tells the story of a class I taught on dating and relationships. The students decided to produce a newspaper entirely devoted to discussing sex and hooking up on campus, and they wanted to pull every person they could into this conversation—students, faculty, staff, administration, and yes, the president. Not only did they find willing and open conversation partners everywhere they looked among their peers, Student Affairs, and Campus Ministry, but twenty-six faculty members (on a small liberal arts campus) from all disciplines, including mathematics and the sciences, agreed to devote some or all of their class time to discussing the newspaper the day it was released. This thrilled and surprised my students. BUT—and this is a big but—the president refused to see them or talk to them about it. His refusal bothered my students so much they kept returning to his office, hoping he would change his mind. They asked for a meeting, wanting to present him with a copy of what they wrote, wanting, in so many ways, his approval—not necessarily of everything they said, but of the effort itself. They'd poured their heart and soul into this paper they offered up to the campus. Full of courage and willing to take this risk, they'd taken all the intellectual and human passion inside of them and bared themselves to their community, in the hope of transforming it for the better. And isn't that what college is for?

The president never came around. He refused to meet with these students who had labored night and day to write smart, honest, respectful, careful, critical, and intellectually astute articles that questioned attitudes about sex and hooking up on campus; he refused to engage with students who were calling for an inter-generational conversation and reassessment of these issues in their community. On the day their newspaper came out, the students left a copy with the president's administrative assistant, hoping that maybe after he'd seen what they'd done he'd get in touch, but they never heard a word from him. Despite all the conversation they generated across the campus among students, faculty, and staff, it nagged at them that the president refused to be part of it. His refusal had the effect of diminishing what they'd done. It was a de facto disapproval of the conversation itself, of the attempt to bring critical discussion of sex and relationships into the classroom, into the daytime reflections and thoughts of his students.

I understand that college presidents have many forces bearing down on them, most of all from boards and wealthy alumni. Many board members and alums are business people who care more about university finances and avoiding scandal, and they may regard sex as a flashpoint for potential damage to the institution's reputation, and therefore a topic to be avoided at all costs. But, regardless of such forces, and whether we like it or not, the president can set the tone for how these issues are dealt with—or if they're swept under the rug. They can be dealt with in ways that are shameful, silencing, and dehumanizing. Or the president of a college can empower the entire university to courageously take up these issues in all their complexity and difficulty.

The faculty come next.

If you are a member of the faculty and you are reading this, you need to realize how much your students appreciate when you open up even a single class discussion to issues related to sex and hooking up and relationships. You need to realize how much they care when you show up to a talk on campus that has to do with these topics and sit among them to listen. Your students notice when you show up to the table for this conversation. They want you there, and they appreciate it when you participate.

Ultimately, this is a book for everyone, because sexual assault and consent are issues that we all need to think about. This is a book for students who have to deal with these issues directly, and it is a book for the people on campus who take on these topics and the education around them (staff in Student Affairs). It is the responsibility of all of us to tackle these issues on our campuses.

But I am talking to you, the university presidents in this country, because you hold so many of the cards and so much of the power to do right or wrong on this issue. Whether you want this responsibility or not, it is yours.

PART I

The Situation on Campus as It Stands

INTRODUCTION
WHEN ASSAULT BECOMES "NORMAL"

In 2006, when I was doing research for a study about hookup culture on campus, I met a young woman named Amy. What Amy told me that day is still vivid in my mind more than a decade later. Her story became a touchstone for me, one I return to often.

Though she was just nineteen at the time, Amy was already a remarkable young woman—beautiful, smart, accomplished, popular—the kind of student every other person on campus wants to be like. She gushed about how much she loved her school, her friends, her classes, her activities. And then she told me about the time she was sexually assaulted. Only she didn't say that, exactly.

What she said was that she'd been drinking and began to kiss a guy, but then had passed out. When she woke up, she discovered that "he was masturbating into my mouth," as she'd lain there, out cold.[1]

Amy told me this like it was no big deal, like it was the kind of thing that happened regularly among her friends. She shrugged it off and then moved on to talking about other things. It hadn't occurred to her, even in the slightest, that she'd been sexually assaulted.

I sat there, sick from the images Amy's story provoked, saddened by the way she breezed past the experience as if it was nothing. How could something that, to me, was a clear-cut case of sexual assault seem to Amy merely another hookup gone awry? Even more worrisome: How could she so easily shrug it off? What about the culture had taught Amy *not* to see what had happened to her for what it was—assault? Could it really be that what happened to Amy was fairly unremarkable among her peers? And what would that say about sexual assault on campus? About our understanding of consent or lack thereof?

While Amy had brushed off what happened, I couldn't help but fixate on the word she'd used to describe what this young man was doing while she lay there unconscious: "masturbating." As though he were alone, as though Amy, a person, a human, was really an object, a sex toy at his disposal, there only to get him off, to be used for his pleasure. The fact that she was passed out and unresponsive didn't seem to be a concern for him—it just meant that she couldn't tell him to stop.

What was it that allowed him to see Amy in this way? To diminish her value, her humanity, her agency so completely? What was happening on this campus, in our culture, that would make this young man ignore the fact that Amy did not, *could* not, consent to this encounter? What enabled him, *empowered* him, to enact such violence upon another person? Did he even know that what he was doing was violent? What about the role of alcohol in this assault? How do we comprehend and evaluate it, and how, if at all, does its role complicate our response?

I've never stopped thinking about Amy, nor have I ever stopped thinking about the young man she was with that night. More recently, I've started to wonder whether Amy would recount her story differently today. With everything that has happened of late with Title IX and the national effort to talk about sexual assault and consent on campus, would Amy now know to name her experience as an assault? I've also wondered if the young man who committed this act of violence against her would now realize what he had done, too—if today he would recognize himself as a perpetrator, as someone who'd committed a crime.

One thing is clear to me: what happened to Amy (and it indeed happened *to* her because she was unconscious) should never happen to anyone. It is an assault, by definition, because she could not consent. Amy was the first person I interviewed to report a sexual assault, but she was not the only one, and over the last ten years many young women (and some men) have told me stories about sexual encounters where consent was murky at best, and obviously absent at worst. The sexual assault problem lays bare a kind of sickness infecting higher education, one that involves people of all genders and sexual orientations. Until recently, it has festered largely under the surface despite the best efforts of those who've tried to make people, especially the people in charge, sit up and take notice. What we have is a crisis in which college students are committing sexual violence against their peers without worrying about the consequences for themselves or their victims. But constitutive of this crisis is the fact that colleges have been looking the other way for decades.

Rape Culture Is Real

There is a lot of debate about rape culture, both in general and at colleges and universities. Is it real? Or is it some hysterical accusation made by extremist, man-hating feminists? By people who are in denial about the realities of desire and want to turn innocent encounters into criminal actions? People who see all men as sexual predators?

Rape culture *is* real.[2] And there is no clearer evidence for it than the fact that college students like Amy learn to shrug off assaults as though they are normal. When dozens of Hollywood actresses accused Harvey Weinstein of sexual assault and harassment, the floodgates opened, and the #MeToo movement was born.[3] These events also made it clear that enduring assault and harassment is a regular part of what it means to be a woman in our culture, a common feature of American workplaces, present in every profession imaginable.[4] At the moment, it seems as though we cannot go a single day without another famous, powerful man being accused by multiple women of sexual assault and harassment. In the space of just a few weeks in the fall of 2017, Russell Simmons, Louis C.K., Charlie Rose, Matt Lauer, and others have fallen after women came forward to accuse them of various unwanted sexual acts and attention. This list could go on and likely will go on long after this book is published.

Around the same time, controversy erupted after it was revealed that Congress has been using taxpayer dollars to broker secret settlements on behalf of members accused of sexual harassment and assault. The *New York Times* reported that since 1997 there have been 260 claims of sexual misconduct and that more than $17 million has been paid out to victims.[5] Representative John Conyers, Congress's most elder statesman, "retired" after multiple accusations of sexual harassment from former staffers were made public.[6] Senator Al Franken resigned after similar reports. This, too, will surely continue.

It appears we have arrived at a pivotal moment with regard to rape culture, sexual harassment, and sexual assault. From one angle, it looks as though we are beginning to realize that rape culture is real, to reckon with it and dismantle it. But from another, it seems as though the only looking going on is looking the other way. Even as so many powerful men are being held accountable for past actions, the president of the United States has been accused by more than a dozen women of some form of sexual assault or harassment, and he has been recorded on tape joking about how he enjoyed sexually assaulting women, how he can just "grab them by the pussy" whenever he feels like it. By occupying the highest office in the land, Donald Trump conveys to the entire country that sexual harassment and assault not only are acceptable but are part and parcel of what it means to be a real man. Trump has sent the message to our country (and the world) that all it takes for accusations of sexual harassment and assault to go away is a flat-out denial that these acts ever occurred, as though the denial itself can erase the acts and the suffering of the women who have come forward with accusations. By sneering at these women and what they've claimed, Trump has sent a countermessage to everyone who has been watching these powerful men fall: disregard and dismiss the accusations and the women who make them, and we men can keep the status quo safe for us now and into the future.

Until recently, many women on college campuses have also been discouraged from coming forward with accusations of assault and harassment, even from reporting violent gang rapes that happened while they were passed out from drinking. Bringing such accusations would result in terrible reprisals, as women have long known. The culture has been such that women must contend with the possibility that administrators, boards, and alumni might be more interested in protecting the rapists and a school's reputation than in helping them file a complaint, seek justice, get help, and find safety.[7]

The culture within higher education has likewise arrived at a pivotal moment with regard to rape culture. Schools are moving toward dismantling a culture of impunity toward harassment and assault because of Title IX, which is forcing schools to own up to and correct past negligence. But despite Title IX's focus on consent education and sexual assault prevention in higher education, colleges and universities have a long way to go before they can honestly say they support a culture that is challenging—and ideally transforming—rape culture. The shift in higher education, much like the one occurring in the workplace and the media, has also been highly uneven. Counterevidence is also reported regularly.

In the fall of 2016, for example, the *Wall Street Journal* reported on a string of sexual assaults committed by members of the football team at Baylor University—an athletic powerhouse and America's largest Southern Baptist university—and the various ways the head coach, assistant coaches, athletic department administrators, and even the university's president covered up seventeen accusations of assault committed by nineteen members of the team, including two instances of alleged gang rape.[8] Seven Title IX claims were filed against Baylor, charging that there was institutional collusion to cover up assaults, a cover-up that was intended to protect the football players who participated in these assaults and the football program along with it, and that stretched all the way to the president and board members. When news of this broke, Baylor's president, Ken Starr, its athletic director, Ian McCaw, and its Title IX coordinator, Patty Crawford, were all forced to resign. Art Briles, the football coach, was fired. A member of the Texas House of Representatives suggested that it could be one of the worst college athletic scandals of all time.

But the fact that it was seen as a *sports* scandal is itself telling. What about the way it reveals how people in power at Baylor buried evidence of sexual violence against women to protect a culture that celebrates violence and aggression off the field as well as on? It seems as though people were more interested in the impact of these assaults on Baylor's football program than in how they affected the women who were assaulted. It is indeed a scandal when a college dismisses sexual violence as something other than what it is (boys will be boys, some people seemed to be saying). Such dismissals glorify the most reprehensible, patriarchal norms of masculinity, enabled by the inexcusable behavior of men at the head of prestigious academic institutions. What happened at Baylor is an example of rape culture in action, and it is also evidence that an institution will still collude to protect rapists rather than help victims, because money and football are deemed more important than women's safety and well-being.

The fate of Title IX is uncertain with Betsy DeVos now at the helm of Trump's Department of Education. DeVos has already rescinded the two major sets of guidelines for Title IX issued by the Obama administration, which attempted to use Title IX to reduce sexual assault and harassment on campus (more on this in Chapter 1). The Trump administration, via DeVos, released its own revised set of guidelines in September 2017, muddying the waters even more with respect to what Title IX now means on college campuses, and how effective (or ineffective) it will be in tackling systemic sexual violence within higher education.

Much about sexual assault and harassment is in flux.[9] The only thing that is certain is that by the time this book sees the light of day major changes will have occurred yet again. This new reality raises even more questions about where campus culture will go with respect to these issues, and where society will go along with it. Will we come down on the side of dismantling rape culture and the systemic sexual violence on campus, or on the side that Trump boasts about, which involves blatant denial and sweeping these issues back under the rug?

A Personal Note on Title IX

I have my own history with Title IX.

When I was in graduate school in the 1990s, I was sexually harassed for well over a year by one of my professors. After many months of silence, then trying to tolerate his behavior, and then trying to put a stop to it on my own, I came forward to my university. First I told a professor, then the chair of my department (who soon became the dean of the school). My chair immediately sent me to the office at the university that handled complaints of sexual harassment. I told the woman in charge about the situation, and she told me that a letter would be written to this person requiring him to stop contacting me, and that there would be consequences for his behavior. I would soon receive a copy of this letter, she said.

The professor's behavior continued, and I went back to this office on three more occasions to report it. Each time I was told the professor would be dealt with, that there would be consequences and a letter, that I would get a copy of the letter, and that this woman would follow up with me to confirm that action had been taken. When, after the first and second meetings, I did not receive copies of the letters or any further communication, I went back to talk to this woman, and each time she told me it must have gotten overlooked or lost in the mail and that I would soon receive my copy. I believed her each time, believed that she wanted to help me. It took me several months to realize that my university did not plan on helping me, that it was most interested in my silence, in my going away. I had trusted in this woman and in my university completely—and I came to feel that I had been wrong to be so trusting. It was a terrible lesson for me.

It wasn't until my dean (also my former chair) recommended that I get a lawyer that it occurred to me that I might need one. He said it had become clear to him that the school was not being straightforward with me on the three occasions when I went to make a report, that in fact, it had done little and had no plans to do more. He had come to believe that the only possible way I would get the university to do anything was to make a legal threat. I was stunned to think that a university could behave so negligently toward a student, toward *me*, that this would be required. But I did get a lawyer, begrudgingly, because I had become desperate for this professor's behavior to stop and extremely discouraged that my university had failed me.

The lawyer helped me file a Title IX complaint with the Department of Education. Only after this complaint and another complaint with the Equal Employment Opportunity Commission were filed did my university begin to listen and take effective steps to ensure that this man's behavior stopped.

If I had not gotten a lawyer, that would not have happened. And even with a lawyer and my Title IX complaint, very little was done anyway. There were no formal repercussions for the man who had harassed me for more than a year. I bore the brunt of everything, and the only real actions taken, other than a small financial settlement and written assurance that the professor was receiving counseling, involved steps such as renegotiating the terms of my graduate program's requirements so I would not have to take another course from him to complete my program, or have him sit on my dissertation committee. At the time, my primary concern was to make sure he would never contact me again, and at least my Title IX complaint accomplished that much.

But the fact that I filed a Title IX complaint means that I, too, am like so many women students on campuses all over the United States. I, too, am like so many women students who have realized that the only way to make their school care about what they've suffered is to resort to threats of legal action and public scandal.

This reality that I lived, the fact that I, too, have a Title IX complaint, that I was forced to file one because of the disregard of my university, saddens me still, as I am sure it saddens and maddens my peers who share this same unfortunate distinction. This part of my history cost me a lot back then, and I am still living the consequences of it in the present.

But the fact that I have a Title IX complaint in my past also tells us something very disturbing. My claim was made back in the

1990s and is now more than twenty years old. This means that people, young women like me, have been filing Title IX complaints about harassment and assault for decades, but only very recently have schools begun to pay attention. Only in the last few years have people become outraged about this situation, because certain representatives in Congress and the Obama administration, quite literally, made a federal case of it.

And I have thought lately, on a number of occasions: I am a part of Title IX's history. It is a strange and unpleasant history to be a part of. Growing up, I thought of Title IX as a beautiful thing, a glorious opportunity for my generation of girls and women. It meant we could play sports; it meant that I grew up, like many other women my age, as an athlete. I am a part of Title IX's history in this way as well. But Title IX has a dark underbelly, one I didn't know about or understand until I needed to, and now I have the misfortune of being a part of *that* aspect of Title IX's history, too.

The other thing I can't stop thinking about is this: If I too filed a Title IX claim, how many other women of my generation did as well? Of earlier generations than mine? How many more of us are out there?

I think it is difficult for people who have never been at the mercy of their institutions in this sort of way, who have never had to use Title IX under such terrible circumstances, to understand the despair a person goes through, to have to pit oneself against a giant when one is small and young, to stand up to the institution in which you put all your hope and trust, in which you invested your future and your dreams—and to do so alone. To feel that you have no other option because you did your best to exhaust all other options first.

So, in this regard, with respect to Title IX and our conversations about sexual assault and harassment on college campuses, I am both an insider and an outsider. I am an insider because I was once a student forced to file an accusation. But I am also an outsider, a researcher who is trying to come to terms with what is happening right now, inside our campus gates. As so many of us are, I am trying to come to terms with Title IX's present, both its value and its limits as a tool for preventing sexual assault. For me, Title IX was *an* answer, but an imperfect one. It was not *the* answer—and we shouldn't try to make it the only answer now.

When a student has to turn to Title IX for a school to be willing to take real action, to pay attention to what the student has suffered, it means that the school has failed at an essential task, one at the very heart of what it means to be a university.

The Missing Piece in Our Conversations about Consent on Campus

One point of this book is to examine sexual assault and consent on campus and the current efforts to educate members of campus communities about these issues. To do that requires us to ask questions about the purpose of the university within culture and society. It also requires us to consider the cultural constructions of masculinity and gender biases operating in society that contribute to the existence and perpetuation of sexual violence in general. But another of the points of this book is to focus on the dominant culture and attitudes about sex that students inherit when they set foot onto their university campuses, which is at the heart of my previous research.

Hookup culture and its accompanying gender and sexual norms will complicate any effort toward consent education at the university level. I believe we need to reckon with this, eyes wide open, or we will continue to fail in our efforts to address sexual assault and to teach consent—something that no community can afford. A culture of hooking up creates the circumstances for the kind of assault that happened to Amy. So many of us have developed blind spots about hookup culture, and refuse to see it as problematic, but from where I sit, the missing piece of the conversation around consent on our campuses is that these conversations have to happen in the midst of such a culture. I want to give that missing piece the time and attention it deserves.

It has become unpopular among feminists to critique hookup culture.[10] But I would argue that it is not only possible for a feminist to be a critic of this culture—it is required. Having spoken to thousands of students over the course of a decade has made me into a critic of hookup culture. It is a culture that disregards sexual agency, desire, and communication. It impoverishes our ability to talk honestly and openly about sex with our partners. It diminishes our capacity to be truly liberated and empowered because it restricts choices, forcing everyone to conform to the dominant model of sexual behavior. To educate effectively around consent requires us to reckon with hookup culture, especially if we are feminists. Having heard so many young women describe the negative effects of this culture on their lives and brush off assaults as if they are no big deal has convinced me that hookup culture goes against everything I've ever learned about feminism, and certainly everything I've learned from feminism about sexual assault and consent.

In this book, I will also address the ways in which we are currently educating about consent in response to Title IX, in order to expand how we think about that education. I spent six years working in Student Affairs and Residence Life, living on campus among students, working with resident assistants in the dorms, and overseeing exactly the kind of education and programming that falls to professionals in these fields. Right now, the lion's share of the burden of consent education is still falling to Student Affairs people—typically only to them. This is a failure on the part of our campus communities. It's not a failure on the part of the Student Affairs people. They've been put in an impossible situation: tasked with educating an entire community about sexual assault, harassment, and consent, with effectively dismantling a culture that permits and perpetuates sexual violence on campus, but with only a small fraction of the people in charge paying attention to their efforts.

Sexual violence is systemic. The response to it needs to be systemic as well. It cannot be addressed by attending to the surface of it—the words "yes" and "no" that students are supposed to use in situations of sexual intimacy, taught to these young men and women by programs Student Affairs imports from outside the campus. Colleges and universities might claim they are trying to address sexual misconduct on campus, but then they dump the entire problem on a few people (some of them students themselves), who are not given the necessary time, space, personnel, or financial resources to begin to tackle systemic sexual violence and harassment in our communities.

The result is that we talk only about the *how* of consent and not the *why* of it—*how to* consent, but not why anyone should care about it in the first place. We are offering band-aids to communities in need of major surgery. We are stuck on "yes means yes," invested in making sure college students know that they need to get their partners to say these words. We are not talking about what consent really means, despite the fact that this consent education is occurring in communities that boast about intellectual rigor and about educating young men and women to be productive and respectful citizens of the world.

As it stands, the education offered to young adults occurs at a very technical level. Yet the current crisis has little to do with students not knowing the right words and everything to do with the problematic surrounding culture, gendered norms, and attitudes about sex that make it difficult for students to *use* those words. "Yes means yes" isn't enough because "technical consent" isn't enough—and we shouldn't allow it to be. True consent requires the capacity to read and hear the verbal and nonverbal cues of your partner, but it also presumes that both partners enter a sexual situation with the capacity to value and regard each other as people worthy of the care, concern, and attention that consent requires. Consent goes beyond individual situations of sexual intimacy to a culture where care toward and the valuing of one's partners are givens, where an understanding that consent has something to do with ethics is a given, too. But to get to this place requires addressing the systemic nature of sexual violence on campus and in our communities—and doing *that* requires a gargantuan effort by all of us, not just a few of us. It means a university must go above and beyond the legal minimum required that allows it to check a box for the government that says, yes, we taught about consent.

That we are allowing a literal, technical definition of consent to suffice reveals that sex talk at our universities is tragically impoverished. Teaching the technicalities of consent at a one-time campus event cannot turn the tide of a culture where young women have learned to shrug off assault, and where (at least some) young men have learned that the best course of action in the face of a passed-out female peer is to have sex with her unconscious body.

But shifting beyond the *how* of consent toward the *why* of it forces us to think about consent in a broader, more systematic, and communal way, and it forces us to reckon anew with the idea of the university itself. We must become critical thinkers about these subjects and address them with the language of ethics, of right and wrong. We must call on not just a few members of the community to take up this task but on as many as possible, all the way up to the university president and, yes, even the board.

To accomplish this requires all the resources a university has to offer. It requires that a college community rethink its tenure requirements and the ways these requirements may make it difficult, even impossible, for faculty to prioritize teaching and writing about these issues. It requires universities across the United States to grapple with how biases about academic worth and rigor may delegitimize the classroom conversations necessary to teach about consent with the depth it requires; how these biases, in turn, devalue the personal lives and experiences of students in such a way that they learn to divide their minds from their bodies, their critical thinking skills from their nighttime activities. We need to do the exact opposite of this, turn these biases on their heads, if we want to address sexual assault and consent on campus.

Despite the abysmal records of our colleges and universities on sexual assault, it is my belief that tackling systemic societal problems like sexual violence goes to the heart of what higher education is about. It is an opportunity for American universities to show their mettle. Universities claim to be powerful forces for good in our world and for the good of the young people within them. It's time they started acting like it.

TITLE IX

A CRASH COURSE

We are living in a new age, one in which Title IX—a law passed by Congress in 1972 that, until recently, was most commonly associated with gender equity in college sports—has become a tool in the fight against sexual assault. Title IX is now a go-to resource for students with claims of assault and harassment, especially if their universities seem to be turning a blind eye to the accusations. It is also the driving force behind newly revamped sexual assault education aimed at helping students understand the nature of sexual assault and consent.

This initial shift in focus occurred in 2011, when the Department of Education's Office of Civil Rights sent out a "Dear Colleague" letter to all institutions of higher education. "Sexual harassment of students, which includes acts of sexual violence, is a form of sex discrimination prohibited by Title IX," the letter states. "In order to assist recipients, which include school districts, colleges, and universities (hereinafter "schools" or "recipients") in meeting these obligations, this letter explains that the requirements of Title IX pertaining to sexual harassment also cover sexual violence, and lays out the specific Title

IX requirements applicable to sexual violence."[1] This letter was, in effect, a new interpretation of Title IX that brought sexual violence directly underneath the umbrella of what counts as sex discrimination.

Then, in 2013, President Obama signed into law the Campus Save Act, which requires institutions of higher education to teach everyone on campus—not just students, but faculty, administration, and staff as well—about sexual assault prevention, domestic and dating violence, sexual harassment, and stalking.[2] It was also in 2013 that two former University of North Carolina students featured in the documentary *The Hunting Ground*—Andrea Pino and Annie Clark—filed a Title IX complaint against their university and began helping women on campuses all over the United States to use Title IX to file complaints against their own institutions. Senators Kirsten Gillibrand of New York and Claire McCaskill of Missouri took notice, and soon college sexual assault was on Congress's radar. It took all of the above for people across the country to finally realize how common it is that college students (particularly male students) perpetrate acts of sexual violence, and talk of rape culture has come to dominate conversations about campus life.

Stories that were widely covered in the media have not only raised public awareness about this issue but also forced universities to take the problem more seriously. (They have no other choice: as of January 2017, more than three hundred institutions were being investigated by the US Department of Education for their handling of sexual assault cases.)[3] Title IX has become an enforcement mechanism that requires institutions to respond to students' claims and punishes them with costly investigations and, potentially, the withdrawal of federal funding if they fail to do so adequately. Fear of public backlash is a powerful motivator.

All of the preceding, as well as subsequent "Dear Colleague" letters from the Department of Education under the Obama administration, have provided a wake-up call to schools that had previously done little about sexual assault and harassment on their campuses. Maintaining the status quo might suddenly become very expensive and very embarrassing. Because I speak frequently about sex on campus, I've had a front-row seat for the uptick in university interest in sexual assault. Institutions across the country suddenly wanted to find people who could help them comply with Title IX because the price of not doing so has gotten very high.

What compliance actually means was clarified in a "Dear Colleague" letter issued on April 29, 2014, an extensive Q&A about how to interpret Title IX for situations of sexual assault and harassment on campus. Before that, schools were essentially flying blind. This 2014 letter spells out in more detail what universities are required to do in terms of resources and procedures on campus (though it does not spell out the procedures themselves). One of its major clarifications was that schools must designate a Title IX coordinator to be the point person for all complaints, and that this person "must be informed of all reports and complaints related to raising Title IX issues, even if the report or complaint was initially filed with another individual or office or if the investigation will be conducted by another individual or office."[4] In April 2015, another "Dear Colleague" letter made clear that having a Title IX coordinator is required by law, and an accompanying "Letter to Title IX Coordinators" delineated this position's responsibilities according to the federal government.[5]

Then, in the fall of 2017, everything that happened under President Obama with respect to Title IX was thrown into question because of the change in the administration and the arrival of Betsy DeVos at the helm of the Department of Education. I will do my best to trace the contours of what happened with Title IX under Obama and then introduce the major ways the Trump administration has altered its reach so far—changes that are still in their infancy as I write this and that will surely change even further in the coming years. The only thing that has not changed between the shift in the administration from Obama to Trump is that the use of Title IX in relation to sexual harassment and assault sparks great controversy and is the subject of enormous debate, as well as a lot of confusion and questions.

Title IX's Reach Is New, but Sexual Assault on Campus Is Not

In the spring of 2015, in response to these Title IX changes, the Association of American Universities (AAU) launched the Campus Climate Survey on Sexual Assault and Sexual Misconduct. The survey was conducted at twenty-seven elite institutions across the United States, including Harvard, Dartmouth, and Yale. It was designed to assess the incidence, prevalence, and characteristics of incidents of sexual assault and misconduct. It also assessed the overall climate of the campus with respect to perceptions of risk, knowledge of resources available to victims, and perceived reactions to an incident of sexual assault or misconduct. Among the findings are that 23 percent of respondents reported personal experiences of sexual misconduct on their campuses, and that, when students were asked why so many sexual assaults go unreported, their most common response was that the issue "was not considered serious enough."[6] Toward the end of the Obama administration, there was talk of the federal government requiring all universities and colleges in the United States to administer the survey to their student populations, but nothing came of that.

With all this public conversation and related change on campus, one might assume that the crisis over sexual assault and harassment on campus is new—but it's not. It's just that the "Dear Colleague" Title IX letters have brought new attention and resources to an enduring problem. That 23 percent statistic found by the Campus Climate Survey in 2015 is one that has held fairly steady for decades—really since Mary Koss, a professor of psychology at the University of Arizona, oversaw the first major study that looked at incidents of sexual violence among college students, and subsequently, people began gathering statistics about sexual violence on campus.[7]

Generally, surveys show that the chances that women who attend college will experience sexual violence is either approximately 1 in 4 (25 percent) or 1 in 5 (20 percent).[8] The Centers for Disease Control and Prevention (CDC) reports that 18.3 percent of women (approximately 1 in 5) are raped at some point in their lives, as are 1.4 percent of men (approximately 1 in 71).[9] Nineteen percent of college women report being victims of rape or attempted rape. These statistics may shift now that there is so much press coverage of and interest in sexual violence and harassment on campus and beyond. New interest in these issues has sparked many more related studies as well as funding to investigate rates of sexual violence and harassment. Just in the last couple of years, major studies have been launched on the subject (though none so big as the AAU Campus Climate Survey), among them the National Institute of Justice's survey of fifteen thousand women at nine colleges and universities, which found the rate of sexual assault on campus to be 25 percent.[10]

While the statistics have remained steady, what's new is that victims of sexual assault and harassment are more aware they can use Title IX to make complaints to their universities, that Title IX dictates how universities must handle these situations, and that the government is holding institutions accountable for mishandling them at a higher level. Victims have considerably more leverage today—the threat of lost federal funding hanging over a university goes a long way toward empowering victims at institutions that previously may have brushed them aside.

There are several reasons why sexual assault on campus may seem to be on the rise, though. I already mentioned one of them, that incidents of sexual violence and harassment typically go unreported, but because of greater public awareness and attention to this issue, more victims may now feel they can come forward than in the past. It's also possible that victims are better able to identify assaults when they happen (and are unwilling to shrug them off any longer). But until very recently, it has been common that the data will show that not a single sexual assault occurred on a given university campus during a particular academic year. Upward of 90 percent of universities and colleges reported zero assaults on their campuses in the year 2015, for example, according to an American Association of University Women (AAUW) analysis of reported data.[11]

People decide not to report assaults for all sorts of reasons—shame, concerns about privacy, the pressure to pretend that what happened was no big deal and move on, the belief that it would be too difficult to prove an assault has occurred, concern about starting an adjudication process one cannot stop, fear of retaliation, and the conviction that others on campus will side with the accused. The Rape, Abuse, and Incest National Network (RAINN) reports that approximately 80 percent of college women who allege sexual assault do not report it to law enforcement.[12] Regardless of how much we, as a society, discuss the problem of victim blaming, it almost always happens once a report is made. This means that reporting assault or harassment carries the potential to be victimized twice—first by the assault, and second by being publicly blamed for it.

One of the most important things this renewed focus on Title IX is doing is changing the climate on campus—or trying to change it—to make it easier for victims to come forward. Title IX is meant to be a tool that both empowers victims to overcome silence and fear and protects those who make accusations from retaliation. The hope has been that Title IX can ultimately be a preventative force on campus, so that students don't have to make claims in the first place. But while Title IX has certainly empowered some victims to come forward, and is forcing institutions to become more accountable to their students (and staff and faculty), the rates of reporting are still incredibly low—between 5 and 28 percent, depending on the university, according to the AAU Campus Climate Survey.[13]

Most of the preceding data focus on women, and that is because men report assaults and harassment at rates that are nearly negligible. Why? Yes, men are surely victimized less often than women. But not *never*. Is there something about our understanding of sexual violence and harassment, the way that we have constructed it, that prevents (or at least dissuades) men from naming it as something that happens to them? What is it about our cultural and societal understandings of masculinity that we pass on to boys and young men that does not allow them to identify and claim this experience? Men on campus are most often viewed as the perpetrators of assault and harassment (because, statistically, this is the case—approximately 98 percent, according to various reports and studies).[14] But as we wonder about the factors that dissuade women so powerfully from reporting sexual assault and harassment, we must consider the cultural and societal factors that make it prohibitive for a man to make such a claim as well. Title IX applies to all students, of all genders, not only to women.

Universities Respond to "Dear Colleague" and Title IX with Mandatory Reporting

Just as there is no unified process for adjudicating Title IX claims, there is no unified program that universities employ to educate their students, staff, and faculty about sexual assault, harassment, and the prevention of sexual violence. That every college does things differently has been a subject of national critique, as has the reality that we are essentially expecting colleges to oversee what are criminal procedures—sexual assault is a crime, yet there is really no one on campus with experience overseeing criminal adjudications. Usually a panel made up of faculty and staff—who, until recently, likely had no or very little training on this issue—is charged with overseeing the process, and sometimes these panels include students. It's not as though there are lawyers and judges handling these claims. These panels typically listen to what the claimants say, hear from some of their peers, and then vote. Colleges are not criminal courts, and they shouldn't aspire to be. Why are we asking them to play this role? There is no doubt that reform is necessary to improve these processes so they do not continue to be sources of further trauma for everyone involved. Examples of institutions botching this process are numerous and have received plenty of attention in the press. One only has to go to the Department of Education's list of colleges under investigation for Title IX to find examples.[15]

Another response to Title IX that has colleges and universities split involves mandatory reporting. Mandatory reporting is a procedure that is now in force on many campuses, but it is often criticized, and I, myself, am against it. I'll provide a hypothetical scenario to illustrate what it is.

Imagine that you are a member of the faculty, and Maria, a student in one of your classes, shows up at your office hours one day. You've gotten to know Maria fairly well over the semester. She's bright and engaged and often comes to you outside of class to discuss readings and ideas for papers. In the process you've gotten to know a bit about her family and home. Usually there's a smile on her face, but today she seems distraught. She asks if she can talk to you, and you immediately know that whatever it is, it isn't the class readings. You say of course, and she sits down; she is quiet for a few moments, but clearly agitated and nervous. When she finally gains enough courage, she launches into a story about a party she went to the night before and a sexual encounter she had, during which she thinks she was assaulted. She obviously feels shame about admitting this, scared to make the accusation, but also worried about not making it because she's traumatized and angry and doesn't want this person to do the same thing to anyone else. But she's also *really* uncertain about what to do, or whether she wants to do anything at all. Maybe, she tells you, she should just let the moment pass and move forward like nothing happened because if she makes an accusation, it will become a big deal, everyone will take sides, and then she'll have to keep living with this night and its consequences forever, rather than just tucking them away and being done with it.

Maria came to you for a listening ear, for a person with whom she can talk things through, for some advice, because she trusts you, and because she needed to get this off her chest to an adult. She's not ready to take any official action and may decide she never wants to.

You, as Maria's professor, listen intently to all she has to say, and your first concern is making sure she has some resources to begin processing what happened and how she feels about it. You begin to offer her a list of people she might talk to, especially someone at the counseling center. You tell her that before she leaves the office you'd like to call the counseling center to see if someone there can see her immediately—in fact, you'll walk her over. You mention medical resources, and you also mention the Title IX coordinator on campus and the possibility of beginning the adjudication process, which is another option for Maria.

Maria shakes her head emphatically at this—no way, no, she's not ready for that. She needs more time to think before she'd take that step, a step that feels huge and potentially very, very public and official and therefore very, very frightening.

But what if your school has mandatory reporting? Well, this would turn out to be very unfortunate for Maria, and likely for you, too, especially if you want to be a resource and listening ear for a student like Maria, if you want her to trust you enough to come to your office and have this conversation with you because she needs someone to talk to.

Mandatory reporting requires anyone on campus—faculty certainly, professional staff as well, but also student staff such as resident assistants (RAs)—to inform the Title IX officer if someone tells them that an assault has taken place, even if the victim begs for secrecy. Some schools are taking this a step further and are reporting these incidents to local law enforcement as well.

So, there you are in your office, listening to Maria, realizing what you have to do, that it's likely going to traumatize and shame her even further. You explain that you are required to report what Maria has told you. She is horrified and wishes she'd never told you anything in the first place. She thought she was taking a positive step by opening up to a faculty member, but now she realizes she's just given all her power away to authorities on campus.

There is plenty of debate in higher education about such policies as well as pushback from faculty and staff in places where schools have adopted such measures (Purdue University is one example).[16] Because so many staff and faculty have ended up in positions like the one I describe here—where they did not really quite understand what mandatory reporting meant until someone showed up in their office, and by the time the faculty member or staff person realized what the student was saying, it was too late to provide a warning of what would be required—schools are becoming very clear about making sure all students, staff, faculty, and administrators are aware of the policy. Universities with mandatory reporting are trying to take precautions so there are no surprises like the one you sprung on Maria in your office. But, of course, that also likely means that if Maria knows about the policy, she might not tell you—she might not tell anyone, for that matter—for fear of triggering a process she isn't sure she wants to be a part of.[17]

Mandatory reporting exists so that colleges can't brush incidents of assault and harassment under the rug as they have done in the past, and can't publish statistics that don't reflect reality—which is meant to be a good thing. But those of us who oppose it worry that informing students about mandatory reporting might indeed convince victims to stay silent rather than confide in a trusted adult. A single report of assault or harassment can throw an entire campus into chaos and turmoil, with the alleged victim and perpetrator at the center of this storm. Accusations kick up all sorts of unexpected, painful, and angry conversations, the possibility of which can be terrifying for someone thinking of coming forward. Because of the shame, uncertainty, and worries about privacy that surround sexual assault and harassment, as well as the concerns about what others will think if the news gets out, as well as possible retaliation against victims (basically, all the reasons that sexual assault is so often unreported), it's no wonder that most people are reluctant to tell anyone about an assault. But if the possibility that telling someone on campus, even one's RA, might trigger a process that victims have no control over, they may be even more reluctant to confide in someone—someone who might direct them to much-needed resources like counselors and medical attention.

Betsy DeVos's September 2017 Changes to Title IX Procedure

Other controversial Title IX procedures involve the makeup of the adjudication panels mentioned earlier, especially the number of people on those panels who need to agree that an assault occurred. A simple majority? A unanimous vote? This issue made news when a Stanford University football player was being adjudicated for assault, and three out of the five members on the panel found him to be responsible, yet the young man remained enrolled in school and was planning to play on the football team again in the fall. After Stanford had spent months in the spotlight because of the widely covered rape trial of another student, Brock Turner, the university was yet again making headlines for deciding that a unanimous verdict was required for a student to be found guilty of assault.[18] (This policy is rare; most universities require a majority.) The debate on this issue revolves around due process for the accused and concern for fairness for the alleged victim, in circumstances that are notoriously difficult to prove. Many advocates worry that to require a victim to get a unanimous verdict constitutes an undue burden.

The adjudication procedure/due process issue is one of the places where Secretary DeVos has enacted the most notable shifts with regard to interpretations of Title IX so far—specifically, the "standard of evidence" that universities use to adjudicate claims of sexual assault. The Obama administration used the "preponderance of evidence" standard, which is a lower burden of proof than the "clear and convincing" standard, which puts far more of a burden on the accuser to provide evidence of sexual misconduct. The September 2017 Q&A document released by the Office of Civil Rights at the Department of Education (under DeVos) allows schools to choose either standard, the argument being that for all other adjudication procedures, schools require a higher burden of proof, so they should not treat sexual assault as an exception to this burden and require a lower burden only for these situations. The Q&A states, "When a school applies special procedures in sexual misconduct cases, it suggests a discriminatory purpose and should be avoided"—discriminatory against the rights of the accused.[19] This change has upset sexual assault advocates deeply because a major reason for using the lower burden standard has to do with sexual assault being notoriously hard to prove because it is usually a "he said, she said" situation, without eyewitnesses. Allowing schools to use a higher burden of proof means that DeVos is restoring things to their pre-2011 standard, which made it very difficult for an accuser to prevail, and which critics believes tilts the favor back toward the accused.

In fact, all the notable changes under the September 2017 Q&A favor accused students in this equation: from opening the time frame for how long an investigation may take, to allowing schools to encourage accusers and accused students to enter into mediation and/or other informal resolutions, as opposed to going through the official adjudication process. In theory, this opens up more options to students, including the person who is bringing the accusation of assault. Yet the concern is that this will pressure victims to opt for an informal resolution as opposed to an official, formal one—that victims will feel pressured by their schools to choose this option—as well as increase the possibility that by not choosing this route, they will face even greater retaliation for going through the official process, which comes with greater potential consequences for the accused.

Title IX: Not an All-Purpose Answer

I remember a lecture visit I did not too long ago, on one of the campuses embroiled in a national scandal that was receiving daily news coverage. I'd just arrived at the school and was unsure where I was supposed to meet my contact person. As I wandered around, heading in and out of buildings—the student center, the library, and even the lobbies of a few residence halls—I noticed something on the walls with direct relevance to my talk that evening. Posted in just about every hallway, practically everywhere I turned, were giant posters, framed under glass, with lengthy instructions for how to give and gain consent for sex.

The posters seemed to have been written by a group of lawyers who'd never had sex. They presented a number of steps—maybe ten—for gaining and giving consent that seemed directed at robots, not human women and men. What was immediately clear, and what depressed me most, was that this was obviously a big part of this university's response to the sexual assault scandal.

The school was checking off boxes—forcing the students, literally at every turn of the hallway, to confront completely unrealistic expectations for consent. The reason, I suspect, was so the school could say it had fulfilled its obligations, so it could prove to the public, to anyone, that it had informed everyone of the expectations around consent. The plethora of giant signs would allow the school to pat itself on the back and say, "Phew, we got that job done, so hopefully we won't lose our government funding. Now, when a student comes to us with a complaint, we can honestly say that we were very clear about what consent is. We can tell the media that we have signs about exactly what consent involves everywhere you look on campus, so the students should have known better."

Title IX requires consent education, and, sadly, a lot of the current consent education looks similar to what I have just described. While I am heartened that we are finally taking sexual assault seriously, I worry that the conversation we've had so far is overly legalistic. Title IX has been an important factor in bringing these issues to the fore, but it is not an all-purpose answer to the problem. For one, Title IX's expectations are still too vague, and very much still in flux. There are no standard procedures; people's rights (or lack thereof) are unclear because the situation is confusing. And while new attention on Title IX's relevance to sexual violence has put colleges and universities on notice, ultimately, Title IX should not be the focus of the conversation. The focus should be on consent much more broadly.

Title IX should remain a last resort for the people who populate our campuses. When a student, or anyone, has to reach out to Title IX for help, it means that we have failed—in our efforts at education, at understanding the complexities of human sexuality, and at preventing the tragedy of sexual violence and harassment. But I worry that Title IX is becoming the catch-all for how we deal with sexual violence at our colleges and universities, allowing everyone to not really deal with the sources and structures of sexual violence on campus that create it, enable it, and perpetuate it.

Another complicated issue has to do with the campus Title IX coordinator. All schools are now required to fill this position, yet schools are still figuring out what a Title IX coordinator does and who is qualified to be one. The position is still in its infancy, which in one respect, given the recent developments regarding Title IX, is understandable, but in another can be disastrous, since this person is responsible for ensuring that both victims and accused students are treated fairly in a high-stakes process involving a felony crime. Some institutions have done special hires for a Title IX coordinator, and some have appointed an individual who already works on campus, say in Student Affairs, to take on this job in addition to the full-time job they already hold. Certain colleges and universities designate an almost random person, say, an administrative assistant who has no training or interest in sexual assault prevention, to be the point person to deal with these issues. These schools are checking off a box for the government rather than sincerely trying to address the problems of sexual assault and harassment within the community.

In my experience visiting campuses, shortly after the first "Dear Colleague" letter was issued in 2011, I would meet the person who had recently been designated the Title IX coordinator, and usually he or she had no idea what it meant to be one or what the job encompassed. When I asked coordinators what they thought they were supposed to be doing, often I got a shrug followed by an answer such as "Nobody really knows."

More recently, since the federal government issued specific guidelines and expectations for this position to clarify this person's role and responsibilities, schools have begun taking the Title IX coordinator job seriously: coordinators attend conferences to try to figure out how to handle their jobs and what their jobs entail, and schools are investing more in these people by creating paid, full-time positions. But I would say that most of the Title IX coordinators I've met are not envied by their colleagues. In fact, the position is regarded as a nightmare job. It is extremely controversial, high-profile, and always one campus misdeed away from potential scandal. Few people are adequately prepared for such a job, but someone has to do it so schools can check that box.

Another problem related to Title IX is very basic: most students have not read their college's sexual misconduct policy. Even if it's posted in every hallway, that does not mean that everyone on campus has taken the time to stop, read through it, and understand its legalese. Many students, including those who have attended whatever Title IX–related education their institution mandates, and even if their school also requires a human resources–like online tutorial about consent and the school's policy, have no recollection of ever having seen the policy.[20] Resident assistants have usually read it because it's been handed to them during RA training, and they are expected to help enforce it—even though they are students themselves, struggling with expectations around sex and hooking up on campus like everyone else. There is a general disconnect between students' experiences and the policies we are developing on campus. Unless a school goes out of its way not only to ensure that students read and discuss these policies but also to answer students' questions about them, most students won't read (or perhaps even look for) the policy in the handbook until they find out they're in trouble for violating it, or if they become the victims of sexual violence and wonder what recourse they have.

These policies tend not to be preventative; in other words, they are punitive. Policies can only be put toward prevention if we—all of us on campus, not just someone we import to talk to first-year students at orientation—actually have discussions with our students about them. We should talk about the policies in our classrooms, post them on our syllabi, and connect those discussions to students' real experiences and, where possible, relevant readings that we are teaching in our courses.

When I have passed out copies of a university's sexual misconduct policy in my own classroom (policies have grown lengthy and complicated of late), students tend to grow wide-eyed as they read through it. It stresses them out to see how complex the policy is, to take in all of its clauses and its legal-sounding jargon. Actually reading the policy, slowly and thoroughly, in a way that allows students to comprehend some of what it says and implies for their social, party, and sex lives, takes time, effort, and a willingness to field and discuss their questions and concerns. Most faculty (and staff, for that matter) either do not feel qualified to discuss this policy or do not consider it relevant to the classroom or their subject, so it is usually left entirely outside the academic conversation—a grave and costly mistake, in my opinion.

In her polemic *Unwanted Advances: Sexual Paranoia Comes to Campus*, Northwestern University professor and far-left feminist Laura Kipnis delivers a scathing critique of new interpretations of Title IX under the Obama administration, after she was brought up on Title IX charges for writing "Sexual Paranoia Strikes Academe," an article published in the *Chronicle of Higher*

Education in 2015. Kipnis's article discusses a Title IX case of sexual harassment against one of her university colleagues and—in her irreverent, mocking style—expresses an eye-rolling disapproval of how Title IX infantilizes students, criminalizes student-teacher relationships, and assigns an inordinate (and false) level of power to the professor. *Unwanted Advances* is her response to what she went through because of Title IX, with Kipnis slamming both the law and how it's being carried out on her campus and others, in particular the secrecy surrounding who is doing the accusing, what exactly the accusations are, and the fact that the accused are expected to not discuss the Title IX complaint against them with anyone, effectively placing a gag order on the accused. At various points she calls the Title IX adjudication process a "witch trial" and an "inquisition." The secrecy is meant to prevent retaliation against the accuser on campus, yet Kipnis's objections regarding her own experience of how she was treated at Northwestern make a compelling argument—aside from the sarcasm that permeates her prose, which is in poor taste. Rather ironically, Kipnis has become a bit of a darling on the right for *Unwanted Advances* and her many articles and commentaries against Title IX, despite her extreme left, feminist leanings. In another layer of irony, she was the subject of a second Title IX complaint on her campus as a result of the book itself. Both Title IX cases against Kipnis ultimately came to nothing, and she was cleared of any violations. Her story certainly paints this contemporary iteration of how Title IX is used on campus in a decidedly negative light.[21]

Yet, as imperfect and insufficient as Title IX and its related policies may be, we also need them. We need to pay attention to the tremendous backlash against the Obama administration's use of

Title IX to address accusations of sexual assault and harassment, usually made by women, and what it tells us about our societal and cultural biases about gender and sexual violence. We seem to want to be able to shrug off these reports (though perhaps, since the accusations against Harvey Weinstein and other public figures, things are starting to change). Considering due process in light of Title IX *is* important, though even with Title IX and all the press and scandal it has generated across the nation, it's not as though young adults (most of them young women) are coming forward in droves to report each and every assault that happens on campus.

Dealing with an assault, considering reporting it, is like standing before a massive wall with spikes all across its face—it's going to be a long, difficult, frightening, and painful climb. Scaling that wall is so intimidating that most victims decide to remain silent. To report an assault is to court vicious hatred (particularly online) and more threats of sexual violence. When you are already suffering deeply, why would the promise of more punishment and public humiliation and attacks by your peers seem appealing? Or even endurable?

When President Trump appointed Betsy DeVos as secretary of education, she immediately began to talk about limiting the reach of Title IX in addressing sexual assault and harassment on campus (and it's no wonder this was her priority, given the president's own proclivities). The angry outcry of people who claim that Title IX paints all men as perpetrators is more important to this administration than trying to address the systemic sexual violence to which (mostly) young women have been subject for decades, without any recourse or resources. I believe that we, as a society and culture, need to look long and hard at what we are teaching the young women in our care about the way we value or don't value them. We are telling them, implicitly, that the ideal response to an experience of assault is to shrug it off, to understand that, once again, this is just "boys being boys." To not brush off an assault is to court public punishment so severe it might feel worse than the actual assault itself. To report an assault is to make oneself the subject of public ridicule and to enrage a powerful faction of conservative forces that will rain down vicious attacks.

All this to say that, yes, Title IX is making a dent (or trying to) in the systemic sexual violence that pervades our communities of young adults and that particularly affects young women. But the backlash against it far outweighs its successes. The reality that Title IX involves legal recourse and an adjudication process is still too intimidating for the average victim to make use of it, leaving the majority to remain silent. Title IX is one small piece of the puzzle, but not the most important one, and not the most effective one.

Consent and education around it constitute the umbrella conversation we need to be thinking about. Consent involves far more than the Title IX–required student handbook definitions of "affirmative consent," amusing educational skits at one-time events in auditoriums packed with students, and words like "yes" and "no." Legalistic posters in every hallway will do little to reduce sexual assault; they are there to protect the institution more than its students. And while most institutions are making an effort to fulfill the educational requirements of Title IX in addition to the legal ones, the typical approach that most schools adopt is inadequate, which is the topic we'll turn to next.

2 | THE STATE OF CONSENT EDUCATION

Showing How Much You Do Not Care (and Do Not Understand Consent)

In the fall of 2014, I was on a lecture visit in the Midwest, having dinner with some students who'd come for a conversation about the climate around sex, dating, and hooking up at their university. Over pizza, the students tried to explain life on their campus.

"When you're hooking up with someone," said one young woman, "it's, like, a competition not to care."[1]

"It's, like, whoever can care the least about the other person wins," another followed up.

As we sat there, eating our pizza, two of the students, both young women, set their plates aside and got up out of their chairs to mime the way they communicate this lack of care for their partners. One of the young women turned her back on us, then looked at us over her shoulder while flicking her wrist like she was brushing away a gnat and said, "I don't care about you! I don't care about you!" Meanwhile, the other woman did the same thing: "Well, I don't care about you either!"

Everyone laughed, the two young women included, and they sat back down to continue dinner and our discussion about why it was so essential to convince a partner that you are uninterested—even if deep down you are actually in love with that person and want to be in a long-term relationship. During a first hookup, they explained, you don't know what the other person is thinking, and you definitely don't want to be the one to give away what you're thinking and feeling because that would tip the balance of power in the other person's favor, and maintaining power is key during a hookup.

It's clear to everyone on campus, according to these students, that even if you aren't indifferent toward a person or toward sex, even if you are the exact opposite of indifferent, you are supposed to act casual. Nobody wants to be considered clingy, whiny, needy, immature, or high-maintenance, and the students have imbibed that caring about someone and conveying this during a first hookup risks all of these—and, worse, subsequent rejection by that person and ridicule by one's peers for not being able to shrug off a partner. The women especially do not want to be seen in these ways because everyone assumes that women already are high-maintenance, needy, clingy, and so forth. Thus women have to work extra hard to overcome the stereotype.

But these students interpreted the perceived campus-wide requirement to act casual during a sexual encounter as literally turning their backs on their partners, regarding their partners with derision (at least, performing this derision), and conveying to their partners that they are so worthless they can be flicked off one's shoulders like pesky gnats. The students continued their jovial conversation about how you would progress from "I don't care about you" during an initial hookup toward a more substantial relationship. This involved maintaining this attitude through many more hookups, and likely also study dates and coffee dates (though you would never call them "dates" to the person you are dating-but-not-really-dating), where you both hang out but continue to act like you don't care if you ever see each other again when you say goodbye, even though you are dying to see them and be with them again immediately. This is College Courtship 101 today. My dinner companions kept laughing as they explained these things, aware that the whole charade doesn't make any sense and doesn't get them what many of them often want from their hookup partners, which is a relationship, or at least not quickly.

This wasn't the first time I'd heard a conversation like this, but it was the first time I'd heard students talk so directly about the importance of convincing their partners that they could not care less about them, even if there was much laughter across the table. It was nervous laughter, and also a knowing laughter, because the students knew how contradictory their words sounded. When they want something more from their partners, they have learned to mock these feelings, to be ashamed of them. They know that to admit you care means that something is wrong with you. You have failed at having sex during college.[2]

So, there was a level of self-awareness among the students that they are contending with a paradox. But there was a complete lack of self-awareness that the conversation they were having had everything to do with consent and sexual assault.

To enter into a first-time sexual encounter with a partner by imagining turning your back on that person, expressing that you do not care about them and that the other person is worthless, is not exactly a recipe for consent. To me, this is obvious. But thinking about these things is part of my job. The problem is that this is not at all obvious to the students. It doesn't occur to most college students to consider the context in which they are having sex, or the structures around it that may or may not establish sexual norms and attitudes that are problematic for consent. It doesn't occur to students to critique, evaluate, and assess the narratives like the one they offered me that night, asking how those narratives might lead to sexual violence by discouraging communication during sexual intimacy.

The next evening, I asked a different group of students on the same campus if they agreed that hookups were a "competition to see who can care the least." "Yes" was the resounding answer. Then I asked them to tell me what was behind this attitude.

"Because when you care about someone, you risk getting attached, so you risk getting hurt," said one person. "It's all about protecting yourself."

"If you let yourself care about someone, you give them all the power," offered another, reflecting this concern I'd heard discussed at length the night before. "And no one wants that."

Risk. Attachment. Hurt. Self-protection. Power.

These are all potent forces in sexual relationships. The way students raised these topics implied fear, anxiety, and a sense of helplessness when it comes to sex. It implied an implicit understanding of how difficult it is to control one's emotional responses in the context of sexual intimacy—which is what makes them feel such fear and powerlessness. There are risks in caring, and taking such risks can be scary. No one wants to feel pain. No one wants to get hurt. Being vulnerable can be frightening. But in the effort to avoid getting hurt, a lot of people can end up getting hurt terribly and suffering deeply.

"What about sexual assault in all of this not caring?" I asked the students next. I had been thinking about this nonstop since the night before.

No one spoke, and no one seemed to have any answer.

It had not occurred to these students that in their disregard for one another in situations of sexual intimacy, in their attempts to show how little they cared about their partners on behalf of this self-protective impulse, they might also create circumstances in which consent falls by the wayside; that, in ignoring their partner's feelings, they might not notice when that person says no or stops actively participating in the encounter; that, in other words, they might not notice the moment when the care-free hookup turns into an assault, or when consent becomes very, very difficult to determine.

I am telling this story not because I want to shame those students about their lack of enlightenment—far from it. Sex, sexual identity, sexual decision-making, love, relationships, and all the attendant emotions are some of the most complex aspects of our humanity. Philosophers, novelists, poets, theologians, politicians, scientists, educators of all kinds, and theoreticians of all stripes have puzzled over, reflected on, written about, discussed, worried over, legislated around, composed poetry about, and conducted research and experiments on these topics in an effort to better understand this part of who we are.

How can we expect our college students to grasp even a tiny slice of this complexity when we've barely talked to them about sex and love during their young adult lifetimes? When they likely have never engaged in an intellectually rigorous discussion about these subjects in a classroom? Thinking through the role of consent and the potential for sexual violence in the cultural script students inherit for having sex and hooking up at college requires a level of critical awareness and self-awareness about sex that we— their parents, high school teachers, and faculty and administration on campus—do not offer them and maybe don't even realize they need. And the average sexual assault and consent education occurring on college campuses at the moment doesn't begin to approach the in-depth conversation students require, one that will empower them to unpack, critique, and become more self-aware about the operating cultural narratives at their schools with respect to sexual assault and consent.

We have our work cut out for us, and we're only just beginning.

"Affirmative Consent" Policics and Education

When I was in college in the 1990s, consent education didn't exist—or if it did, I didn't encounter it anywhere, not in any organized way. I was handed a rape whistle at some point, though, about which my roommates and I joked endlessly. I believe the whistles were handed out only to women. One of my roommates would occasionally blow hers in the house to get our attention or to indicate that someone was supposed to do the dishes or vacuum the living room. We obviously did not take them seriously. How can you when they're just handed out with a bunch of other stuff, like a souvenir keychain and a baseball cap? Plus, the notion that we would actually wear these whistles around our necks to parties and while having sex seemed ludicrous (I believe they were bright yellow, or maybe they were bright blue with yellow letters printed on them). They would make us look and seem ridiculous, and the idea that we would use them in the middle of unwanted sex seemed even more ridiculous, as if at some point we'd say, "Hey wait a minute, let me get out my rape whistle."

The comedian Sarah Silverman even has a hilarious list of "Ten Rape Prevention Tips" for men, number 9 of which is: "Carry a rape whistle. If you find that you are about to rape someone, blow the whistle until someone comes to stop you."

I suppose the whistles were meant to provide protection against an assailant who might jump out of the bushes. But I did go to school during a time when people had started to talk about date rape, and somewhere, somehow, I grasped the notion that "no meant no" and I could employ this "no" whenever necessary. Meaningful dialogue about sex on campus, however, was something I did not encounter back then, nor would I have known where to go to find it. "Consent" was not a regular word in my vocabulary, or in the vocabularies of my friends, either.

We've come a long way from handing out rape whistles and leaving students to fend for themselves. Most people have shifted from a "no means no" approach to sexual assault prevention education to the more sex-positive language of "yes means yes."[3] The hope is to shift the burden of prevention off of women, who are typically expected to be the ones to say no. This shift is also an effort to move conversations about sex on campus away from the overly simplistic—"Danger! Sex can be traumatic, violent, and also give you diseases! That's all we've got!"—toward more optimistic conversations about healthy relationships that also attend to consent, sexual assault, bystander education, sexual health, and pregnancy prevention.

Jaclyn Friedman and Jessica Valenti, coauthors of *Yes Means Yes: Visions of Female Sexual Power and a World without Rape*, have been at the forefront of this effort, as have many other feminist activists who have pushed colleges to become more sex-positive in their education and to stop acting as though women are in charge of preventing their rapes and the rapes of friends. There has been a tremendous and necessary outcry from many corners to address men and "toxic masculinity" as bearing responsibility for rape prevention, since men are overwhelmingly the perpetrators of sexual assault. Princeton University recently went so far as to hire a new staff person whose title is "interpersonal violence clinician and men's engagement manager," to great controversy and a lot of resistance from certain factions on campus and conservative media (I present more on men and masculinity in Chapter 5).[4]

But the fuel propelling this movement is, of course, Title IX, which requires education about consent. Many secular colleges and universities, as well as many main-line Protestant and Catholic institutions, have chosen to use the "affirmative consent" model as the "highest standard" for educating their students and for updating their policies.

To take one example, SUNY, the state university system of New York, defines affirmative consent as follows:

"Affirmative consent" is a knowing, voluntary, and mutual decision among all participants to engage in sexual activity. Consent can be given by words or actions, as long as those words or actions create clear permission regarding willingness to engage in the sexual activity. Silence or lack of resistance, in and of itself, does not demonstrate consent. The definition of consent does not vary based upon a participant's sex, sexual orientation, gender identity, or gender expression.

Some universities' policies allow for both actions and words as forms of consent, but others require ongoing verbal consent. In 2014, the State of California passed an affirmative consent law, SB-697 (known as the "yes means yes" law), that requires all public and state institutions to enact affirmative consent models at their institutions. The law defines "affirmative consent" similarly to SUNY and other schools:

"Affirmative consent" means affirmative, conscious, and voluntary agreement to engage in sexual activity. It is the responsibility of each person involved in the sexual activity to ensure that he or she has the affirmative consent of the other or others to engage in the sexual activity. Lack of protest or resistance does not mean consent, nor does silence mean consent. Affirmative consent must be ongoing throughout a sexual activity and can be revoked at any time. The existence of a dating relationship between the persons involved, or the fact of past sexual relations between them, should never by itself be assumed to be an indicator of consent.

These definitions typically do not end here but instead expand to enumerate a variety of further points, many of which go into detail about the relationship between alcohol and consent. The policies tend to be both specific (sometimes enumerating how much alcohol a person can consume before he or she cannot, by definition, give consent) but also vague. They do not, for example, specify exactly what ongoing consent looks like, much to the chagrin of some of the students I've spoken to, who want things to be spelled out clearly.[5]

The other common approach is the one Harvard adopted in 2014 (to much controversy and disappointment from those in favor of an affirmative consent policy), which imposes an "unwelcome conduct" model that doesn't mention consent. Harvard's policy—which is currently under review—reads as follows:

> Conduct is unwelcome if a person (1) did not request or invite it and (2) regarded the unrequested or uninvited conduct as undesirable or offensive. That a person welcomes some sexual contact does not necessarily mean that person welcomes other sexual contact. Similarly, that a person willingly participates in conduct on one occasion does not necessarily mean that the same conduct is welcome on a subsequent occasion.

It goes on to elaborate in more detail, including the method for determining whether the conduct was unwelcome and all the parties involved in deciding this ("Whether conduct is unwelcome is determined based on the totality of the circumstances, including various objective and subjective factors"). It also emphasizes that a person who is incapacitated by drugs or alcohol cannot also invite "the conduct" and that a "Respondent" (the accused person) cannot use his or her own impairment as an excuse for not realizing that a person did not invite "the conduct."

Some universities, like Columbia in New York City, have chosen to go above and beyond the basic outlining of their policies by providing a plethora of accompanying links to resources for victims. Columbia developed an entire website devoted to consent education, sexual assault prevention, and its accompanying programming, services, and resources on campus, under the heading "Sexual Respect." The reach of this website and their programming around this subject in the community intends to be extensive, and they even produce posters, door hangers, and bookmarks that students can distribute around campus and in their residence halls that are devoted to education about "sexual respect," what it is, and what it means to give and receive it. Columbia's explanations of its policy are more thorough than at most other universities, with links to an in-depth, forty-page online booklet that defines its policies and aims to anticipate and answer any questions that students might have about Title IX, sexual assault and harassment, their rights, the adjudication procedure, and campus resources of all kinds available to both victims and alleged perpetrators. The effort, forethought, and resources that went into developing Columbia's website are beyond impressive, and other universities should consider using it as a model for efforts toward this end with their own communities and students.[6]

It must be noted, however, that Columbia went to such lengths only after it was mired in one of the worst national scandals around sexual assault and university negligence, which burned through the media for nearly two years. During the academic year of 2014–2015, Emma Sulkowicz carried her mattress around campus to protest what she considered Columbia's negligence regarding her own complaints of sexual assault by one of her peers. Sulkowicz received a massive amount of media attention for her protest, and, consequently, so did the university, almost all of it negative. Sulkowicz's situation and Columbia's response became a national model for university negligence and failure on every level to sufficiently attend to students with respect to sexual assault.[7] Surely, the school's new website and current investement in education around this issue is a direct response to this scandal and an effort to counteract so much negative press.

Once universities have revamped their policies, the next step is to explain it to students, all faculty, and staff.

A typical consent education program on a college campus involves a mandatory one- to two-hour event during first-year orientation: upward of hundreds or even thousands of first-year students packed together into a giant auditorium for skits and jokes that aren't all that funny. One of the most popular go-to programs is called "Sex Signals," which deals with consent, bystander education, and other related topics, mainly through humor. Another, more recent, program that is gaining in popularity is called "Party with Consent," which was started by Colby College graduate Jonathan Kalin and aims to teach students about consent at the place where consent is most often at issue—at a party where alcohol is served.

One of the most promising and widely adopted programs is the bystander education efforts that some universities are adopting (the Green Dot program being most notable among them), which train volunteer students in how they can step in and help peers in vulnerable situations at campus parties. The idea is to educate students about their responsibility as citizens of that community to work to prevent sexual assault from happening by making sure that a friend who is passed out from drinking gets home before anything terrible happens, or to intercede if they notice that someone seems to be preying on a drunken peer. Appealing to the wider student population, asking them to step in on each other's behalf and become leaders for prevention, is an excellent move forward, and it does begin to conceive of consent and sexual violence prevention as communal and justice-centered in nature. But these programs have also come under tremendous criticism for putting the responsibility for sexual assault prevention in the wrong place by suggesting that students should take it upon themselves to help their friends and stop rape from happening, rather than targeting prevention efforts where it really needs to happen—with the perpetrators.[8]

While these programs and others like them are at least something, they are definitely not enough. There are also numerous problems with such methods, not the least of which is that a single, one- or two-hour session involving the entire first-year population gathered in an auditorium can't scratch the surface of the complexity of sexual assault on campus or explore the nuances of sexual intimacy and consent. Another problem is the intense focus on words, often exclusively, as constituting consent—the expectation that clear consent requires spoken communication. That legalistic policy written on posters and hanging up all over the campus I mentioned earlier relied on students uttering very specific words at every juncture of a sexual encounter from beginning to end so that neither person would doubt that consent had been granted or was being revoked. But human communication happens in many ways, not just with words, and especially with the body.

Communication during sex is myriad. It can be playful and fun, it can be simple and straightforward, it can be offered with enthusiastic facial expressions and happy sighs, or it might be conveyed through specific requests. Consent can be a nod, a movement to pull someone close, a caress, a look. Plenty of affirmative consent policies do acknowledge and make room for consent through gesture, body language, and other modes of communication. The University of Iowa policy, for example, says that "sexual consent is when both partners agree to engage in sexual activity. Consent should always be mutual, voluntary, enthusiastic and given without pressure, intimidation, or fear." It goes on to say that consent "can be expressed either by words or clear, unambiguous actions."

But in the flurry of our efforts to educate and prevent not just sexual violence but also more lawsuits, government investigations, and public scandals, we risk conveying to students a kind of "avoidance of trouble" model for consent—as in, if they want to avoid being assaulted or being expelled, they should start learning to seek consent according to university lawyers' definitions. Many colleges and universities seem to have decided it's simpler and easier to stick with one type of consent (verbal), and require it for everyone, to teach their students that verbal statements are the only true means to assure consent has been given, rather than deal with the messiness of what it means to be human and the many ways we can communicate around sex.

Consent Is Something We (Often and Also) Do with Our Bodies

Back in the 1990s, Antioch College in Ohio adopted a consent policy that gained widespread national attention—most of it in the form of ridicule (it was even mocked on *Saturday Night Live*). It was dubbed the "Sexual Assault Prevention Policy" and was more popularly known as the "Ask First" policy. What's remarkable is that this policy now appears to have been ahead of its time. It looks a lot like the affirmative consent policies of today and even addresses consent in the context of drugs and alcohol. What made the policy so famous (other than its sheer existence on a college campus at a time when no other schools had them) was the notion that the partner initiating the sexual intimacy had to gain verbal consent at every stage. "Asking 'Do you want to have sex with me?' is not enough," the original policy states. "The request for consent must be specific to each act." The policy required the initiator (at least in theory) to ask for consent to every single thing—which is what led to so much ridicule. Some of the Antioch alumni are feeling vindicated now.[9]

My objective is not to argue against the notion that verbal consent is the only true form of consent. But I worry that this notion is unrealistic on two levels. First, communication around sex on college campuses tends to be poor in general—not only do students struggle to communicate and have hang-ups and fears about communicating, as I recounted at the start of this chapter, but hookup culture is one that privileges noncommunication. After all, what better way to signal a casual attitude toward your partner than to ignore him or her? Because students are often afraid to challenge these established norms—they fear rejection but also wider social implications—campus culture does not support open and mature communication about sex. At least, not yet. This, of course, does not mean that we should give up on teaching students to become better at communicating with their partners—we absolutely should teach verbal communication as central, even ideal, especially when it comes to hookups because the lack of a prior relationship makes other forms of communication unreliable. But without also attending to the peer culture in which students are immersed, we're asking them to thwart established norms without really considering how difficult it can be to do this, and many students don't have the necessary emotional and social courage. We're setting them up to fail.

Verbal consent policies also assume that everyone knows exactly what they want in sexual situations, which, of course, is not always true.[10] A sexual encounter can be a fact-finding mission with one's partner, and it can result in a bevy of confusing feelings about one's desires and interests. Learning to communicate better, and building intimacy and trust, can help a great deal toward talking through what is working, what isn't, and where to go next. But again, on college campuses, the typical context for a first-time sexual encounter is a hookup where often there is no prior intimacy or trust. And we must acknowledge how college students already practice consent (or don't).

Kristen Jozkowski of the University of Arkansas is the premier researcher in this area. Jozkowski has challenged the prevalence of policies that teach that true consent can be only verbal, arguing that such policies have been established by universities and the State of California without looking into the lived realities of how people actually negotiate consent. This failure to contend with reality can limit the effectiveness of these policies, especially because one's ability to offer verbal consent is often influenced by gender and because our culture discourages young women from enthusiastic "yeses" altogether.

According to Jozkowski, in the sexual scripts that young women and men inherit, women are expected to refuse sex, and men are expected to verbally and physically push past women's refusals. Women who give an enthusiastic "yes" run the risk of getting labeled sluts, while men are socialized to discount women's "nos" as "token refusals" they need to turn into nonverbal acquiescence. To expect women to say "yes" enthusiastically, so that consent is crystal clear, is to ignore the power of these scripts. And it is unrealistic to ask young people simply to change these scripts without first transforming the problematic culture that creates them. Only the hardiest of them can swim against such a strong current.

Cultural biases work against women in the other direction as well. Short of a woman aggressively and forcefully exclaiming "No!," men are expected to proceed as far as they can get. "When women are not aggressive in rejecting sex, not only are their partners likely to misunderstand their desires," writes Jozkowski, "campus discourse may suggest that they did not do enough to 'prevent the assault.' This can lead to internalized self-blame, prevent reporting, and perpetuate rape culture."[11]

Scholars Melissa Burkett and Karine Hamilton agree with Jozkowski, and argue that while women should be empowered to say no or yes to sex, gender imbalances and inequalities exist in college culture that limit women's being listened to and respected.[12] Worse still, women learn that any "no" should come with an explanation for *why* they are saying no—such as "I can't tonight because . . . I have my period"—so as not to seem rude. An aggressive "No!" challenges traditional gender norms for women, turning a sexual encounter into something awkward and uncomfortable.

Jozkowski worries that, while affirmative consent policies have good intentions, they simply may be ineffective. They don't consider the cultural biases and scripts around gender that may impede students from taking up certain words, phrases, and emotional attitudes in sexual encounters. "Campus climate is that thing that needs to change," Jozkowski writes. "While students need to be involved in this shift, those at the top (including campus administrators, athletic directors and coaches, faculty and staff, and inter-fraternity and PanHellenic councils, etc.) need to take the lead. And in order for them to demonstrate a genuine commitment to eliminating sexual assault, strong campus-level policies need to be in place, and violations of those policies need to result in serious repercussions."[13] One of the most worrying problems with consent education, according to Jozkowski, is how it still puts the burden on women to prevent sexual assault by asking them to become more "sexually assertive" (yes means yes!) and to protect themselves and their friends through bystander education programs and personal safety programs. Jozkowski is in good company when she also argues that these efforts, though well-intentioned, take the focus off the perpetrators of sexual assault.

While it's possible to change cultural attitudes over time, affirmative consent policies run counter to the scripts young adults inherit about gender norms and hookup culture. If we don't engage students in sustained conversations that help them to analyze, evaluate, and critique these norms and narratives (not to mention the ways in which gender, sexual orientation, race, economic background, ethnicity, and religion operate and are expressed within these narratives and norms), our policy and education efforts will amount to little. But most institutions have yet to find new and creative ways of having conversations about consent. They simply haven't devoted the required resources and time to prevention and education programming. And many schools simply don't know how to tackle it adequately. Instead, they focus on government compliance and avoiding scandal.

The lack of depth in these conversations extends to related areas as well, such as the connection between drinking and sexual assault, which I will address next.

3 | DRINKING ON CAMPUS AND SEXUAL MISCONDUCT POLICIES

Worried and Confused about Drinking and Sex

When I had my students at Hofstra University read the school's policy on consent, they were concerned about the alcohol clause that falls under the heading "Student Policy Prohibiting Discriminatory Harassment, Relationship Violence, and Sexual Misconduct." "Depending on the degree of intoxication," the policy states, "someone who is under the influence of alcohol, drugs, or other intoxicants may be incapacitated and therefore unable to consent."

My students were worried about what that means—exactly. They wanted numbers: How many drinks, exactly, can a person have before consent is off the table? How do you know where the line is? And who decides? Does one person always have to remain sober, so they can determine if their partner is too drunk to consent? What if both people are drinking and have sex? Does that make both partners vulnerable to assault?

Of course, drinking on college campuses is already a difficult subject. Technically, it is illegal for underage students to drink, even though it's also widely accepted that most students will drink regardless of the law. Underage students have already learned that drinking must be a clandestine act, which makes it doubly complicated for campus administration, staff, and faculty to openly discuss students' drinking habits on campus—and for students to discuss their drinking habits with us.

That day in class with my students, I explained that the policy doesn't state an exact number of drinks because everyone is different—height, weight, tolerance, context (is the alcohol consumed over dinner?), and timing (over how long a period is the alcohol consumed?) all affect a person's level of intoxication. This stressed my students out. Because the consequences for running afoul of this policy can be dire—assault, trauma, expulsion, jail time—they wanted clarity.

Some students, faced with this ambiguity, will assume that all drinking is unsafe. And no doubt some people would applaud that stance. But it should actually worry us—not because students are concerned about drinking in relation to sexual assault (we do want them to think about this) but because it's overly simplistic and unrealistic. We need to talk to our students about the nuances of drinking and consent. If we want them to become conscientious adults, such conversations are essential.

My Hofstra students are not alone. During recent visits to a range of campuses, I've fielded many questions from students (especially student staff) on this subject. In response, I've spoken about the relationship between drinking and sexual assault, especially binge drinking, because perpetrators seem to believe that a passed-out body is theirs to have sex with as they please, and there is a high correlation between binge drinking and assault.

But I've also found myself talking about how it is possible to drink and have consensual sex—because it is. I've decided that it's better to be open with students than to pretend that drinking and sex are never a part of life, or are somehow criminal by definition. (Laura Kipnis suggests that these policies risk criminalizing drinking—and I worry that she is right.) By enacting policies that associate drinking with assault, schools inadvertently make it seem as though respectable, mature adults don't ever drink and have sex. But, yes, adults meet up, drink, and have sex all the time—consensual sex. So it is possible for college students to do the very same—which many do. And if students would like to drink, I would like them to learn how to drink as mature adults who do not have a drinking problem.

Drinking does lower inhibitions, but it does this in both victims and perpetrators. It can lower the self-awareness of both parties, making them less likely to have a good sense of their surroundings, which certainly puts students at risk of someone taking advantage of them. But drinking does not cause an assault—a perpetrator causes an assault. What drinking can do is set up conditions where an assault may be more likely to occur, conditions that favor perpetrators of sexual violence. But creating policies that associate drinking and assault does little to address the propensity of a perpetrator to enact sexual violence on another person who also happens to be drinking. Alcohol does not create that propensity. Rather than addressing the root causes of sexual violence, many colleges are instead choosing to try to treat the likely circumstances of it, one of which involves the presence of alcohol.

A recent trend is for universities to enact a ban on hard liquor as another avenue for tackling the problem of sexual assault (in addition to the problem of binge drinking). Stanford University did this in August 2016, after the high-profile scandal surrounding Brock Turner. Dartmouth had already done this at the outset of 2015 as a response to the hard-partying culture on campus, which began to draw criticism for its association with sexual assaults. Just one month earlier, in December 2014, the University of Virginia did the same after it fell under the pall of a fraternity gang rape scandal described in the now infamous *Rolling Stone* article, which was later discredited.[1]

But criticism abounds about such policies as a way to curb the number of assaults on campus: these policies seem to blame sexual assault on the alcohol itself and on the students who drink it, rather than on the person who perpetrates the assault. It is true that alcohol—whether in the form of beer or hard liquor—is more often present than not when sexual assaults occur on campus. And the statistics around assault and drinking on campus are stunning to behold, as is the association of binge drinking and assault (upward of 80 percent of campus assaults involve alcohol). But these statistics do not prove that drinking *leads to sexual assault*. That is a logical fallacy.

These statistics do prove that the kind of drinking that happens on campus puts students, particularly women, at risk for sexual assault; that the way drinking happens on campus turns students, particularly men, into perpetrators. What we are failing to deal with adequately at our universities is the nature of drinking on campus and what this has to do with creating the circumstances that lead to perpetrators committing sexual violence. But the alcohol itself is not the perpetrator of assault, nor is the drunkenness of a victim. Bans on hard liquor fail to address the real culprit of sexual assault, which is the person who commits it. And critics of these bans argue that they are just another way of treating the symptoms that accompany assault, rather than treating the root causes.[2]

But the message and response we offer to the relationship between alcohol and assault cannot amount to implying that a person who drinks cannot give or gain consent, period—because this is just not true. It is true that an unconscious person cannot give consent (and it saddens me that we need to teach this fact, which should already be obvious to students on our campuses). But you can be tipsy, you can be drunk, and you can still give and gain consent. People do it all the time. Just as parents and married people and partnered people and all sorts of people drink and have consensual sex, so too do lots of students. Drinking does not turn a sexual encounter into an assault. Neither does being drunk. Drinking can of course complicate the communication of consent with one's partner—of this, we should all be aware, and it's essential to discuss this with young adults. Drinking to the point of passing out renders one incapable of consent, by definition. But drinking (in general) doesn't prohibit consent. Being drunk and having sex does not by definition make something an assault. We need to level with our students about this and have a deeper conversation about drinking and consent.

The relationship between binge drinking and sexual assault is undeniable, and sometimes the response to this has been to tell women to stop drinking (or, at least, drinking so much). Writers have been called "victim blamers" and even "rape apologists" for suggesting that it is irresponsible for campuses not to educate women about the connection between binge drinking and sexual assault.[3] Critics say these writers are once again placing the onus on women to prevent men from committing sexual assaults. But this view has also rendered nearly any conversation about drinking and sexual assault taboo—which is also unacceptable.

We must look closely, unblinkingly, at the relationship between drinking and sexual assault. We must deal with the fact that drinking on campus, binge drinking in particular, turns some women into sexual assault victims *because drinking also turns some men into perpetrators*. We must ask: Why is it that drinking lowers some men's inhibitions in such a way that they commit assaults? We need to address the issue of binge drinking in general too: Why do any students feel the need to drink to the point of being incapacitated? But simply adding clauses to our sexual misconduct policies will not fix the situation, because it will not stop perpetrators from committing assaults.

The Relationship between Alcohol and Agency: "It Was the Alcohol (That Did It)"

We also need to be talking with students about the relationship between agency and drinking. Why are students so eager to cede their agency to alcohol? Why is drinking to such excess so appealing? We need to ask ourselves: Why has drinking until we pass out become what is also considered "a good time" on campus? Why is binge drinking synonymous with college? And why is drinking prior to sexual intimacy so common, almost as though alcohol is one of its essential ingredients?

When I was doing research about sex on campus, the association of alcohol and hookups was prominent, one of the norms of party and hookup culture. And in a way, this proved to be the case during my research: at evangelical colleges where drinking on campus was prohibited, hookup culture simply did not exist.[4] But on every other type of campus, students spoke at length about the relationship between alcohol and hooking up, especially about "pregaming," which refers to drinking at home or in the residence halls before going out to a party. Amy, the student whose story I told in the introduction, also spoke about pregaming when I interviewed her. She said it was just part of how people got ready to go out, and to go out to drink even more—often much more. Drinking and having a good time go hand in hand, and students absorb this lesson from social media and popular culture even before they arrive on campus. Drinking and college parties have been synonymous in popular culture at least since the film *Animal House*.

Many students think of drinking quite literally as a form of liquid courage to help them approach someone they are interested in. But students also drink to forget—the stress of their everyday lives, the pressures they feel around schoolwork or at home. Sometimes when students speak about drinking, they sound like tired, middle-aged adults who come home from a hard day at work and need a drink (or six). Sometimes alcohol helps students gear up to do something they don't want to do, or something they're uncomfortable with—which should raise major red flags about consent.

But many of the students I've interviewed and spoken to over the years use alcohol as a means of ceding sexual agency, of ceding responsibility for their actions during a hookup.[5] Students talk about weekend cafeteria brunches where everyone sits around gossiping about the craziness of the night before, how drunk everyone was, and what everyone did while they were drunk. Alcohol is an excuse for laughing off one's actions at a party when you're doing the debrief of late-night debauchery over eggs and coffee and rubbery cafeteria pancakes the next day. These drunken activities often include a hookup. Sometimes students don't quite remember what they did because they drank so much, and they rely on their friends to fill them in. Drinking, especially drinking a lot, helps everyone to pretend that what happened at parties the night before is just a game. "Oh my god, I was so drunk!" students will cackle, to explain almost any behavior of the previous night. *It wasn't me, it was the alcohol that did it.*

Many of the worries about drinking and sex that I've heard students express in relation to new sexual assault policies stem from the fact that the typical college sexual encounter starts at an alcohol-soaked party. Given how much drinking goes on, I think students already know that consent within hookups is often difficult to pinpoint, that they can deflect difficult questions by blaming alcohol, and that many have done exactly this in the past. That new sexual assault policies are forcing students to think about agency in relation to drinking (in general) and specifically in relation to sexual agency is a good thing. We don't want them to blame alcohol for their decisions and for whatever happened the night before, especially if what happened amounted to assault.

Sexual misconduct and affirmative consent policies that address sexual decision-making (or our inability to make such decisions) are attempting to confront the correlation between drinking and sexual assault on their campuses. But adding a policy doesn't address students' eagerness to blame their actions on alcohol, nor does it address the various gendered incentives for them to do so. So we are inserting policies into handbooks without addressing the problems at the root: the norms and scripts operating within students' social lives. Which brings us back to the issue of drinking and sex, and the problematic, disempowering scripts our students inherit from hookup culture.

PART II

Inherited Stories

SCRIPTS FOR HOOKING UP, BEING
A MAN, BEING A WOMAN

4 | HOOKUP CULTURE
EXPECTATIONS OF SEXUAL
AMBIVALENCE

Remember When You Could
Just Make Out on the Dance Floor?

One fall semester not too long ago, I was visiting a small, highly ranked liberal arts college in the Northeast, right when the leaves were turning brilliant shades of orange, yellow, and red. I had the privilege of visiting this beautiful campus because a group of about twenty students and their faculty adviser had invited me to give a public lecture and asked me to join them for dinner and a discussion afterward.

This wasn't just any group of students—these were men and women who'd volunteered to get together once a week, every week, to talk about the state of sex on campus. They read books and articles together, and they invited some of the authors of those readings to speak at their school. By the time I arrived, they'd already met quite often and had developed an easygoing rapport and sense of trust. They had rules: what was said in the room must stay in that room, so that people could feel able to speak freely. As we settled in with our food, the students began to unpack some of the issues I had brought up in my lecture. I listened silently, happy not to be talking for a while, as they jumped around to different topics and laughed a lot—they'd clearly grown close. Then they landed on a subject that sparked all of them to join the conversation. It started with one question—from a young man, spoken wistfully and not entirely facetiously.

"Remember when you could just make out on the dance floor?"[1]

The other students laughed. "Yeah," they sighed.

I looked up from my plate. "What do you mean, remember when? Why can't you make out on the dance floor now?"

"Making out on the dance floor was for high school," one of them explained.

The students went on to wax poetically about the bygone days of high school, when life was easier and simpler, and people could just kiss and dance and then call it a night. Back then, it was permissible to act so sweetly and innocently. They also talked about how "hot" it was to make out with somebody while dancing, and how it was really too bad you couldn't do this anymore—*just* this. I want to emphasize here, because of stereotypes about men, especially college men, that the men in the group were just as frustrated about this as the women were—maybe even more so.

"I still don't get it," I cut in, eventually. "What's stopping you from doing this now, if you like it as much as you say? Can't you just do what you want?"

I asked this because I couldn't help myself, and despite the fact that I knew the answer. All my research about sex on campus shows that college students feel the exact opposite—that they *can't* do what they want, because the norms and attitudes established by hookup culture have a tight grip on their behavior, and to challenge these norms is to court social ostracism. But as I listened to these students, so easygoing and confident as they talked about sex, so open and honest, it was still difficult for me to believe that *these* students felt subject to such norms, that they felt they couldn't fight them, either.

It was the men in the group who burst into the conversation at this point, as though they had been waiting to have just this discussion.

"No," one said, as the rest shook their heads, "you can't *just* make out on the dance floor. I mean, you *can* make out on the dance floor at a party, but if you do, it's a decision to hook up, so you better be ready to go home with the girl you're with afterward."

"Yeah," said another. "If you don't go home and try to hook up with her, she's like, 'What? What's your problem? Why don't you want me?'"

One young man, nodding, offered one of his own stories. "I actually tried to walk a girl home one night after we'd been dancing and making out and having a great time at a party. My plan was to say good night at her door and go home and sleep. But when I tried to say goodbye to her, she was like, 'What? You're leaving? But I thought you liked me?'" He chuckled. "So I kind of shrugged and was like, yeah, I like you. All right, I guess I'll come in, then."

The women faced the same struggle from the other side. The general expectation was for a man to try to get as far as he could with a woman. If two people started by making out, it was assumed that they would go home and hook up afterward. In college, guys were supposed to be sex fiends. So if they didn't want to hook up with you, this meant you were somehow undesirable—a massive insult.

Granted, this didn't mean that you actually wanted to hook up with the guy, the women explained. You just wanted him to *want* to hook up with you.

Hearing this, the guys rolled their eyes, and again there was a lot of nodding around the room. They picked up the thread once more.

"Sometimes we're just *tired*, you know?" one of them said. "Like, we had fun, and now we just want to go to bed and get some sleep. That has nothing to do with whether or not we find you hot or hookup-worthy. Like, maybe we can just pick up where we left off on another night?"

"And the worst part," said the guy sitting next to him, "is that you're really tired, you've been dancing and drinking, you want to go to bed, but you don't want to hurt the girl's feelings, but now you're in this situation where you *have* to hook up. And you just want to get to that place where the hookup can be over so you can go home."

"Yeah," other guys concurred.

"And what is that 'place' where the hookup can be over?" I asked.

"You know, when the guy comes," someone explained.

"Yeah, the hookup gets to be over when the guy comes," one of the girls confirmed.

These comments sparked a good deal of commentary about how it's really important to get that part over with so everyone can go to sleep. A number of the guys then talked about how sometimes it's really hard to come, though, when you've been drinking and dancing and what you really wanted in the first place was to just go home. But then there you are, with this girl who's going to take it personally if you don't, so you have to do your best.

This was the first time I'd heard students analyze hookups in this way. Not the pressure to have them—that I'd heard many times before. Or even the way they made hookups sound like a chore—I'd heard that plenty, too. But specifically this issue of "how you knew when you were done."

Then I asked the next obvious question: "So what about the woman coming? Why can't the sign that makes a hookup a hookup be that the *woman* comes?"

"Because hookups are traditionally about the guy coming," someone said. "Hookups are really for men. Or they're supposed to be."

"And because girls are more complicated," one person said.

"And because, you know, you've been drinking and you're both tired, and you may have just met this girl and, like, you don't know how to ask and she may not know how to tell you, and like, this is just not the setting for it, because everyone just wants to go to bed."

A hookup, they were telling me, is *obviously* just not the setting for girls having pleasure and enjoying orgasms.

At this point, one of the young women in the room turned to me, a knowing smile on her face. "See why we're not allowed to just make out on the dance floor anymore?" she said.

Everyone in the room laughed.

Hookup Culture Is a Culture of Sexual Conformity, Not Liberation

Hookup culture has its defenders, but I've had too many conversations like this one to buy the story that it is a culture of sexual liberation. There is too much "should" and "must" and "have to" and too little sexual agency. Students rarely are empowered to ask themselves, "What do I want?" and "What do I desire?" within a culture of hooking up. Instead, they spend most of their time asking, "What am I allowed to do?" and "What am I expected to do?" Students take the prescribed scripts and narratives that are handed down to them and do their best to perform them.

Occasionally, when I am discussing at a campus lecture how hookups work—drawing out the critique of, resistance to, and dissatisfaction with hookup culture that students express—I will often get a question afterward from a member of the audience that goes something like this: "So what are you saying? That we should go back to the 1950s and its sex and gender norms? That students should date, and girls should sit at home primping and waiting for a man to call?"

This question—and the inevitable snark that accompanies it—makes me want to roll my eyes. The answer is, of course not. Students wouldn't want to go back, and I wouldn't want them to. Would I want them to go on dates if they'd like to? Absolutely, the key factor being, would they like to? If the answer is yes, then I'd like them to get what they want—because they are getting very little of what they want when it comes to dating, sex, and romance at college.

People who haven't sat around chatting with students about hooking up and sex for the last decade don't realize that living in hookup culture is also a lot like living during the 1950s. It is just as much a culture of sexual oppression, repression, and problematic, stereotypical gender norms and expectations—a culture where people feel like they don't have choices. The difference is that the expectations are flipped: instead of prescribing that young adults, especially young women, should not be having sex (before marriage), hookup culture prescribes that they *should*, even *must*, be having sex or something is wrong with them. These are both cultures of *should* and *must* that expect and require conformity to norms and rules over the valuing of sexual agency and freedom. When you start analyzing what students tell you in conversations like the ones I've included in this book, the reality that hookup culture is a culture of sexual oppression and repression, of prescription and performance, even of generalized coercion for both women and men, becomes apparent. What's more, it is a culture that perpetuates the same problematic norms around gender that existed in the 1950s.

Let's think about what the students I just described were conveying and analyze their operating hookup scripts:

1. Students wish they could "go back" to "just" making out.
2. There is no "just" making out at college—making the equation as follows: if one wants to make out, one also has to be willing to follow this with a hookup.
3. Guys "must" pursue a hookup—not because they want sex but because if they don't, women will wonder if something is wrong with them (Why isn't this guy as sexually voracious as "normal" men are supposed to be?). And women also will feel insulted.
4. Girls "must" want the hookup to happen—not because they actually want to have sex but to confirm that they are attractive and desirable.
5. When the hookup ensues—not because both people want to hook up but because this is the script everyone is "expected" to follow—both people will be sure the hookup "can be over" and indeed "has ended" only when the man has an orgasm.

6. Everyone knows that hookups are defined by the guy coming and that they are not about the pleasure and orgasm of the woman because female pleasure and orgasms are too complicated and require more intimacy than the hookup allows. Plus, don't forget, everyone is tired and just wants to go to bed.

How is this a recipe for sexual liberation and sexual agency? Where is the freedom to choose and to listen to one's desires—especially for women, but also for men? The level of obligation on the part of both women and men in this script is astounding; they sound as though they believe they have no choice but to do these things. Whenever these students used the words "I wish" or "I want," they were referring to "just making out." And while making out may be what they actually want, they are not "allowed" to have it. Instead, what follows is all the "shoulds" and "musts" and the performing of scripts handed down by hookup culture. Neither party is really getting or doing what he or she wants or expressing sexual agency. These young adults are performing the "play" of the hookup like the actresses and actors they've learned to be. There is a shift from "I want" to "we must" in their story.

The lack of an enthusiastic "yes!" is evident here, but so is the perceived lack of choice and agency overall. The students spoke— laughing at themselves as they did—of a rather begrudging submission to expected behavior. So, if students are performing hookups to prove they can and to prove that they have fulfilled the norms, scripts, and expectations they've inherited, how does consent factor into this? Are they consenting to the *performance* of "yes"? And is that really consent? Or, because students are acting out scripts and fulfilling gendered and sexual norms, is there a coercive and therefore nonconsensual thread running through the culture? Isn't that the problem we run into when any culture prescribes rigid norms, attitudes, and expectations? A one-size-fits-all sexuality that only fits a very few and oppresses the rest?

If hookup culture indeed has a coercive element embedded within it, then why aren't we talking more openly and explicitly about the ways it complicates our education about consent and sexual assault on campus? Because, at present, the vast majority of our education around consent and sexual assault leaves hookup culture aside. We are trying to talk about sexual assault as if we do not also have to reckon with hookup culture. But how can we not, when students tell stories like these?

The Social Contract of the Hookup: Ambivalence

College students tend to define a hookup according to three specific criteria: (1) that it involves some form of sexual intimacy, anything from kissing to sex (and this definition of what counts as sex will vary according to sexual orientation), (2) that it's brief, and (3) that no one is supposed to get attached. In explaining how everyone upholds this third principle, the one that truly defines a hookup, students often describe how communication during a hookup can be problematic. The more communication that occurs during a hookup, the greater the risk of attachment. Once this happens, you've failed at the whole enterprise. The logic among students often goes: it's best not to communicate much if you don't want to get attached. This is worrisome, principally because it undermines the very notion of consent.

The student story of the hookup where consent between parties is skirted is one I've heard a lot. What is uncommon is for students to reflect on the role of consent during these hookups. Like those students at the Midwestern college who are competing "to see who can care the least"—even though they may care deeply—and the ones who are hooking up rather begrudgingly because that's what's expected, even though they'd often rather make out and then go to bed, most students don't feel ambivalent toward one another, or toward sex. But they do their best to appear this way.

Ambivalence about sex and one's partner is an ideal, a goal, and an expected norm handed down by hookup culture—a script they are expected to perform. When I asked students in a survey how they felt about their hookups, only 23 percent of the respondents said they felt "whatever" about them (41 percent were upset and unhappy about them). "Whatever" was the word that came up often among these respondents, enough that I began thinking of them as the "Whateverists." These were the students who truly seemed ambivalent and, perhaps, the only students I surveyed who were "successful" at living within hookup culture. This small group of women and men was able to uphold the social contract that tells everyone that ambivalence about a hookup equals success; thus, these students seemed to be "winning" in the "caring the least" competition. I have long wondered whether this group is expanding, if students are getting better at ambivalence and at showing how little they care about each other and about sex. Or, instead, are more students becoming better performers of the norms and scripts that hookup culture expects of them?[2]

Men and women also use the word "happens" to describe hookups—a hookup is something that "happens" on campus, and

sometimes it "happens" to you. This term comes up as though neither person has any agency or did the initiating. When telling stories
of hookups, many students won't speak about explicitly choosing or
consenting to their hookups (mainly because, until recently, consent
was not a common topic of conversation on college campuses). These
students speak as though the hookup came out of nowhere and suddenly just "started." Some of this may have to do with a student's inability to recall specifics because of the amount of alcohol consumed; it's
not uncommon for memories of these sexual encounters to be fuzzy.

If pressed about this vague language, these students are not
likely to say that they did not consent or that the hookup involved
unwanted sexual intimacy—it is still rare, even in cases like Amy's,
for a student to refer to a hookup as an assault. But consent is often
difficult for students to point to when pressed about it—both
consent by their partners and their own consent. They speak in
the language of obligation, of following along, of doing what everyone else is doing, of finding themselves hooking up as though
they don't quite remember how or who or what started it—and
they may not. Stories like these are better described as non-stories.
They arise via a culture that provides students scripts they are
supposed to follow without much thought or resistance, a culture
that teaches them that sex shouldn't have an impact on them.

To further complicate the way students struggle to discuss
agency and responsibility, often defaulting to the language of obligation as opposed to the enthusiastic "yes" of affirmative consent,
is the (sometimes vast) disconnect between how they actually
feel about sex, their partners, and their hookups and how they
believe they are supposed to feel according to hookup culture.
Publicly, students often act ambivalent, while privately they feel

the opposite. Students who perform the expected shrug toward their partner may privately hope the hookup will lead to greater intimacy and even a long-term relationship.

Out of 1,010 students at Catholic, private-secular, and public institutions who answered a series of survey questions designed to get at their personal attitudes about sex and hooking up, approximately 75 percent strongly or somewhat strongly disagreed with the notion that hookup sex should be defined as a purely physical experience. And to the statement "The best sex is with no strings attached," 58 percent of respondents strongly disagreed, another 26 percent somewhat disagreed, and only 4 percent either somewhat or strongly agreed. But it is one thing to admit these views in a private, online survey, and something else to own these views among friends and peers who are doing their best to act out the culturally accepted scripts prescribed by hookup culture.

The true "Whateverists" aside, young adults, regardless of gender, seem to wish for a culture around sex that is less disconnected and obligatory and more open to connection, sexual satisfaction, and choice. But they live in a culture that teaches them to thwart these impulses if they want to be considered "normal." They're then left to themselves to live with their feelings of discontent and frustration.

A Failure of Respect for Diversity, Choice, and Consent within Hookup Culture

Hookups have existed in some way, shape, or form for ages—even if we didn't always call them this.[3] But the hookup as we know it today is at the center of many myths that have come to dominate sexual attitudes and practices on campus, despite so much private dissent about them.

The most pervasive of these myths is what I have come to think of as the "hookup-in-theory." This is a sexually exciting and pleasurable encounter with a person, potentially a stranger, that is unfettered and fun, that happens without commitment and without the promise (or burden) of anything more. It occurs because two partners wish to be sexually intimate and for no other reason—desire is justification enough. The expectation of more, of tomorrow, of dinner, of any future (however undetermined) is unnecessary. This no-strings, no-judgment opportunity for sexual intimacy is supposed to be available to everyone on campus, with hookups serving as the great equalizer among all genders and sexual orientations.

In such a culture, men are no longer the sole drivers of sexual encounters, the ones responsible for pushing, for convincing, for setting up circumstances so that women can have sex without commitment and so that they can, too. With the hookup-in-theory, everyone agrees to thwart old-time conventions, to throw off oppressive restrictions around sex in favor of the sheer joy, excitement, and satisfaction of sexual pleasure. This is a culture that is supposed to fulfill the feminist desire for sexual equality, that opens the door to a new world of sexual pleasure and experience, of total and complete autonomy.

Most of the students I've met over the years want to hang on to this ideal. The hookup-in-theory seems like something they'd like to be able to do at least once or twice during their college years. But their experience of the hookup-in-reality tends to be very different from the hookup-in-theory that is the stuff of people's fantasies.

Students want to hang on to their right to enjoy the hookup-in-theory, but they dislike being forced to live in a culture of hooking up. The distinction is essential to grasp.

Upholding the right to hook up is vastly different from feeling caught in a situation where one's only option is to hook up, which is where students tend to find themselves. The hookup has become the gateway to all things, even committed relationships. The "shoulds" and "musts" ascribed to everyone have calcified into required roles that everyone must play. The "we can't" and "we're not supposed to want" and "we have to do this, like it or not" rules of hookup culture have piled up so high that many students can't see beyond them. Within this culture, students' desires are often thwarted, and they are forced to abandon a set of values and commitments they once held dear. A culture of hooking up codifies scripts and pervasive norms for sexual intimacy for an entire community—it enforces a one-size-fits-all sexuality. It narrows (and even eliminates) choice. And it silences the voices and feelings of its participants.[4]

A culture of hooking up also peddles a set of norms that are incredibly narcissistic. It teaches people that the only person who matters when it comes to sex is oneself, that partners are objects to be used and discarded or not thought of at all. Hookup culture assumes that participants shouldn't care about sex or their partners, that it is normal not to care, which means if you do care, you are abnormal. This makes hookup culture self-emptying: it decenters sexual intimacy from the person and tells everyone to treat sex as meaningless. It requires a person to give up his or her own interests in sex and the self-care of the body because it is "normal" to allow another person to treat you as an object for his or her personal use, just as you treat that person as an object in return. This is the bargain everyone is supposed to accept when they set foot on campus.

This means that hookup culture also disrespects and diminishes those who continue to subscribe to certain values and attitudes that contradict hookup culture's norms and scripts. Anyone who can't or won't follow those norms and scripts also risks being seen as unenlightened, old-fashioned, and repressed—an outsider. There is no value more prized on our college campuses than diversity. Yet hookup culture makes a mockery of diversity and encourages the mocking of those who can't or won't perform its norms and scripts.

Hookup culture-in-reality has failed everyone. A culture of hooking up looks very little like the hookup-in-theory. By forcing one-size-fits-all norms on young people, it robs them of the chance to develop a sense of sexuality that fits who they are, that fits their desires, needs, and values; a sexual identity and attitude toward sex and their partners that is truly empowering. Any monoculture—be it one that advocates sexual purity until marriage or one that advocates an extremist version of casual sex—is problematic. It tells people that if you don't fit the norm, then something is wrong with you.[5] The ambivalence about sex and one's partner that young adults inherit when they go to college, and the biases and hierarchies that hookup culture perpetuates, are inimical to a culture of consent.

It is of course possible for two people to meet one night, have a pleasurable, consensual sexual encounter, and then part ways the next day. My intent is not to argue that this is impossible or morally wrong. What I do argue is that such hookups are the exception rather than the rule. And the rule—the culture of hooking up and the norms and scripts that come with it—is a problem.

Hookup culture objectifies partners and turns them into a means to an end. And when we blindly and uncritically follow these objectifying scripts and norms, consent is sometimes disregarded and the risk of sexual violence climbs sharply. We may become too busy turning our backs on one another in this "competition to see who can care the least" to notice that our partner no longer wants to be there.

This also means that the better college students get at performing the norms and scripts of hookup culture, the more trouble they have understanding consent. The better everyone is at fulfilling the social contract of nonattachment, the less likely people are to call an encounter a sexual assault, because they aren't supposed to care what happened anyway. A culture of hooking up assumes that everyone has implicitly agreed "not to make such a big deal" about hookups, even "bad" ones. The performance of the ambivalent shrug becomes paramount, so much so that some students don't realize they've been assaulted, don't realize they are assaulting someone else, or are too ashamed to name an encounter as an assault because doing so would reveal their inability to shrug it off.

Worse still, hookup culture can become something perpetrators of assault can hide behind because its norms of ambivalence can foster silence around coercive sexual situations. The social contract of the hookup—that two people agree to a no-strings-attached sexual encounter accompanied by the effort not to care about one's partner—empowers perpetrators most of all. To speak up about sexual violence is to thwart those rules about having a casual attitude about sex. To speak up about an assault, to name it outright, is the opposite of being casual. It's attaching all sorts of strings to an encounter. So for someone to gear up to make an accusation is no small thing. It amounts to a willingness to overthrow the inherited cultural scripts for hookups, to thwart all those "shoulds" and "supposed tos" and "musts" that everyone is working so hard to perform. The sheer effort it takes to break through these messages and norms on the part of victims is daunting, usually far too daunting, allowing perpetrators to sit there, comfortably, within the protective walls hookup culture has built around nonconsensual sex.

Hookup Culture Is a Regular Shame Factory

For several years I've been teaching a seminar on memoir to college students. The most recent time I taught this course, I included *Just Kids*, on the syllabus, which is a memoir by the musician Patti Smith. My students appeared the day of our discussion red-eyed and weepy, swooning over Smith's writing but, even more so, over the story of her love for Robert Mapplethorpe, how they fell hard for each other at seventeen and shared a lifelong love affair full of twists and turns and complications. But above all else, of devotion. The entire group was in awe of the intensity of Smith and Mapplethorpe's love, the way they abandoned themselves to it and to each other.

"Wouldn't it be amazing to be able to love someone like that?" asked one of my students. "To put love at the center of everything you do and are?"[6]

I agreed and told the students that they, too, could make love the center of everything if they wanted to. But they shook their heads no, which caused me to ask, "Why in the world not?"

"Because love makes you weak," was the consensus answer. Especially during college, especially while you are young, especially while you are near the age of Patti Smith and Robert Mapplethorpe when they met. Love conflicts with professional aspirations, my students explained. Wanting love means you're needy and clingy. Loving someone means you're not independent. You "shouldn't" love someone until you've got everything figured out, after you've moved on successfully from school and are well into your career. Attachment is potentially derailing to one's future and is to be avoided.

Yet my students obsessed over the book and about love in general for the rest of the semester. They spoke of their wish to fall in love with someone and to have someone fall madly in love with them, about their fantasies about what it would be like to feel such grand emotions, to love someone so much that they'd follow them to another city, that love would become the central and defining feature of their lives. They came back to *Just Kids* again and again, and each one of them got teary-eyed about it at least once.

Here, again, is yet another dominant, inherited cultural script full of "shoulds" and "should nots" and "musts" and "must nots." Of thoughts expressed as "I wish" accompanied by "but I'm not allowed to."

What was most notable was how my students resented this situation—much like the students who talked of "having to" hook up. The students in my class accepted that this was their lot, but it broke their hearts to do so—and it embarrassed them to admit that they felt broken-hearted about it. They longed for love, meaningful love, big love, life-changing love—and this longing embarrassed them. They longed for intimacy, for relationship, for romantic connection—which also embarrassed them. It's not as though my students suddenly wanted to give up everything, all their professional dreams and aspirations, to run off with an imagined beloved. But they did relish the idea of loving someone so madly that they might actually want to do this—yet another embarrassing thing to admit. There was shame everywhere in their response to Patti Smith's book—shame about their desires, and then resentment that they had somehow learned to be ashamed of their desires.

Hanna Rosin, in *The End of Men: And the Rise of Women*, prizes hookup culture as one where sexual shame has been conquered. "The most patient and thorough research about the hookup culture shows that over the long run, women benefit greatly from living in a world where they can have sexual adventure without commitment or all that much shame," Rosin writes, "and where they can enter into temporary relationships that don't get in the way of future success."

What Rosin and other defenders of hookup culture—like Kate Taylor, the author of the widely circulated *New York Times* article "She Can Play That Game, Too"—don't acknowledge is that while hookup culture has created a world where pursuit of sexual adventure and (very) temporary relationships are no longer shameful, the shame has merely shifted elsewhere. What happens if you don't feel like having sexual adventures? What happens if you find yourself wanting something different? Talk to college students for a while, and soon it's clear that women and men endure torrents of shame. They feel shame if they're not into pursuing hookups, especially if they're men. They feel shame when they long for something more than hookups. They feel shame when they admit they would like to "go back" to being able to "just make out." They learn to hide that they care deeply about a partner, because they know the game they've agreed to play. Reading *Just Kids* helped the students in my class admit that they would love to experience deep love—but they also knew to be embarrassed about it.

Within hookup culture, great shame exists, just not old-fashioned sexual shame. The shame comes when feelings enter the picture. The same comes when individuals realize that they care more than they "should." The shame comes with being vulnerable, with the capacity to be hurt, to be sad, to want something more. Having romantic feelings and desires, wanting a deeper connection with one's partners, can be embarrassing for the supposedly sexually liberated college student.

In this swirl of displaced shame, the "value" that rises to the top is the notion that, during college, what's "normal" is to do our best to prove—at least on the surface—that our partners are unworthy of our attention and investment. To give our partners too much is to risk being clingy, dependent, and overly emotional, which shows just how badly one has failed at the social contract of the hookup that discourages emotional attachment. What gets lost in this spiral of shame—aside from refusing to see that the shame is still there, amid all this "sexual liberation"—is that through hookup culture and in our defenses of it, we've idealized the estrangement or distance between partners as akin to sexual liberation. Yet it is when we diminish our partners' worth—or when we are trying our best to do this—that we may stop noticing what they are feeling, wanting, or not wanting. And then sexual violence can flourish.

We Need to Foster a New Culture of Openness toward, Respect for, and Reflection about Sex

One spring, I was having a conversation with a group of seniors at a Catholic university. The discussion was informal, meandering here and there until one young woman asked a question: Why is sex any different from, say, holding hands? Why do we make such a big deal about it? She wasn't being facetious. She knew that there was a difference, but she wanted to parse it to better understand it.

So, like any professor, I threw the question back to the group. Why did they think we (as a culture, as a society, as people who subscribe to religious traditions) make sex into such a big deal? Even if we are trying not to? The students hemmed and hawed, and then somewhere in the conversation that followed, I asked them, "Well, what do you guys want from sex? What does good sex look like to you?"

The students were stumped by these questions. What did I mean? they wanted to know. "Just what I said," I returned.

What became abundantly clear was that nobody had ever asked them these questions before. No one had encouraged them to ponder what they wanted from sex, or what they might like to try and why, and what was good and what was not so good, or what were their ideal circumstances for sexual intimacy (I don't mean just a private room and a nice soundtrack—that, too, but also the question of whether this intimacy would occur with a friend, an acquaintance, a stranger, a long-term partner; after a party, while sober or tipsy, etc.). It had never occurred to a single one of these students that they should be asking these questions, or that they were allowed to ask them of themselves and their partners. And when the students admitted they had never thought to contemplate these questions, I encouraged them to take the time to do so, since if they were going to be having sex, they may as well figure out how and in what kind of circumstances they might like to have it, and what good sex might look like for them.

I am recounting this story for many reasons, but most of all because it shows how disempowered college students can be around sex, even if they are having plenty of it, and regardless of whether we buy into the notion that hookup culture is a sexually liberated culture. That it didn't occur to these students to ask what they wanted or what good sex would look like is not a failure on their part—it's a failure of our society, culture, and educational system. It's a failure on our part—teachers, parents, professors, coaches and mentors, and other adult figures in students' and young adults' lives—to check in and encourage and invite the young adults in our lives to ask such questions of themselves and of sex. It's a failure of the way most religions turn sex into a series of don'ts and prohibitions— much like hookup culture does, just in the opposite direction. It's a failure to empower young adults to take charge of their sexual decision-making and to explore their own desires, as opposed to simply adopting whatever is handed down through peer culture.

It saddens me deeply that college seniors who are having sex wouldn't know or feel empowered to ask what they want from it. If they are going to have sex, I want them to enjoy it, I want them to be able to talk about it with their partners, and to give themselves time to figure out the circumstances in which they would like to have sex so they are confident and knowledgeable enough to make sure those circumstances match their desires. It's distressing to watch how disempowering hookup culture has been to the young adults I meet on college campuses, to see the ways in which they feel swept up and trapped within it. If we truly want to open up their options, we need to change our own attitudes about sex education.

Sex education in this country is a partisan battlefield, and our children are the casualties. There is so much fear among parents, religious leaders, and political conservatives about young adults becoming sexually active, and so much anger from the Left and among the antireligious about the other side hijacking sex education, that we end up offering young adults very little that is of value to them. What is missing for so many students I speak to is a basic confidence about sex (regardless of whether they are having it) and the ability to ask questions about what they are doing and why they are doing it. So it is no wonder that a culture of hooking up is the dominant culture awaiting college students when they walk through the campus gates. Hookup culture flourishes because sex education is prescriptive, judgmental, and full of fear. Hookup culture capitalizes on young adults who are disempowered with respect to sex, who have given no thought to and made little investment in thinking about what they want because it's been a forbidden topic, or simply because no one has ever invited them to think about such things. Some of us teach our young people how to have sex—the mechanics of it and the risks associated with it—yet too often without addressing what sex might be for or about, for fear we'd tread into the dreaded territory of religion and sexual ethics, of making sex into something too meaningful. On the other end of the spectrum, we teach our young people all the don'ts of sex, leaving them paralyzed to ask questions or to challenge the rules handed down by campus culture.

By politicizing sex education, we are failing this generation. We aren't teaching them about what sex might mean to them or their partners—which, of course, has everything to do with the kind of story we pass on about consent. The conversation about sex and consent should not take place on a partisan battlefield. It should begin from a place of concern for our children and our students, and not from a place of fear or judgment. One-size-fits-all sexuality actually fits only the very few, while leaving most everyone else sidelined, isolated, silent, and afraid to challenge the status quo. Hookup culture is one such one-size-fits-all culture, and the state of sex education leaves young people ill-equipped to deal with it.

The question becomes: What culture might replace hookup culture on campus? And how do we foster a culture that isn't one-size-fits-all? It's not that all scripts and narratives are bad or disempowering. It's that we need to offer new scripts to replace these problematic ones—scripts that empower students to ask difficult questions, to become self-aware, critical thinkers about sex, as opposed to blind followers of inherited norms. These scripts and narratives must empower them to ask questions about sex: about its meaning and purpose and what they want from it. We need scripts that privilege consent and overturn the propensity toward sexual violence that runs through our culture. We need to begin to construct these new narratives—narratives that open rather than narrow the choices available to young people, to accommodate the diversity of our campus populations. This is a tall order but not an impossible one, and one I will do my best to address in Part III of this book.

5 | MEN AND MASCULINITY

THE PROBLEMATIC RELATIONSHIP
BETWEEN MEN AND SEX

The Value of One Man

Professors who teach in gender studies often joke about why men (generally heterosexual men) don't sign up for our courses. Because men don't know they have a gender is the short answer. Because they don't have to know and they don't have to care would be the longer one—or, at least they didn't, not until recently. Men benefit from a cultural and societal hierarchy that values them (typically white, heterosexual men) above everyone else. The name we give to this fact is "privilege."

The notion that it might be a good idea for men to reflect on the ways in which narratives about masculinity have shaped them has typically gone unexamined. It is one of the privileges enjoyed by men (again, especially by white, heterosexual men) not to bother with such concerns, much as it is the privilege of white people in general to ignore cultural constructions of whiteness.

The benefits to men are obvious—they are inherent in the very notion of privilege. But there are downsides. When men lack the tools to think critically about what it means to be a man, this does them real harm (as it harms the women who run into them).

It tends to trap men in patterns of behavior they don't like, performing inherited cultural scripts for how men are "supposed" to act, which leaves them alienated from their true selves. Men would do well to question these scripts, but doing so comes with stigmas attached. Thinking about gender is considered women's work, and to affiliate with women's work is to "lower" oneself to their level, to surrender some part of one's masculinity. Men suffer privately because of the expectations with which they are saddled, even as they feel powerless to change them.

Make no mistake, though: men have an inordinate amount of inherited power—in every area of society, of course, but specifically on our campuses. And because the status quo for men is not to do much self-examination, often they wield their power without any awareness that they are doing it.

During my first four years of teaching gender studies at a small college, I regularly taught a course called Women and Spirituality. The first semester I taught this course, I had two sections, about sixty students altogether, and every one of those students was a woman. But the second semester I taught it, everything changed. And all it took was one man.

On the very first day of the spring semester, as usual, all the students who showed up for Women and Spirituality were women. Then, as I was taking attendance, the door opened, and in walked a man. Everyone's eyes grew wide, and there was quite a lot of nervous laughter. The young man who'd taken a few steps inside the room looked a bit startled as he took in the fact that everyone else in the room was a woman. Somewhat hesitantly, he sat down at one of the few remaining desks in the circle the students had made. I wrote down his name—we'll call him Anthony. As I began to talk about some of the objectives of the class, he spoke up.

"Um, so this isn't a Spanish class?"

"No," I told him.

Anthony jumped up from his chair. "I think I have the wrong room!" He grabbed his books and fled.

All the women laughed. Now we knew the truth: his presence with us was a mistake. There were some "Oh wells," from the remaining students, and plenty of understanding about why he ran away, but also some disappointment. The general thinking was that it had been nice that a man on campus was man enough to show up for a course with the word "women" in the title. The prevailing view was that, while women would certainly show up for a course with "men" in the title, men wouldn't stoop to the level of gracing a course about women.

At our next meeting we were in for a surprise. Anthony came back. He walked in the door, sat down at a desk, and got ready to take notes. I asked him what had happened.

He shrugged, grinned, and said, "I thought this might be a good place to meet women."

Once again, the rest of the class laughed. I worried a bit that Anthony would fail to take the class seriously, but I also welcomed his presence. And it turned out that Anthony approached the class very seriously. He worked hard, participated regularly, did the readings—he was an excellent student. He was a good listener and fit into the class. He was also, it turned out, one of the best soccer players on campus, and although he may have told his friends that he'd taken my class to meet girls, it also turned out he really enjoyed the class and told his friends this, too.

I know this because, from then on, at least five or six men took my Women and Spirituality class each semester. The first semester this happened, they were all friends of Anthony's, his soccer buddies and a few rugby players to whom he'd recommended it. I ended up with an inordinate number of male athletes—some of the most socially powerful men on campus—taking that class. They also turned out to be dedicated, serious students, respectful of the material and of their women classmates. They made wonderful additions to the discussions.

One time, one of the tallest, broadest-shouldered among them showed up wearing a black T-shirt that said, "This is what a feminist looks like" (I had a T-shirt like this that I wore once in a while to class, and he had found one online and ordered it). He proudly wore the T-shirt all over campus. He ended up writing his thesis on gender and wore the shirt to his defense. Our lively discussions and reflections about gender broadened each semester to include perceptions and critiques of masculinity. All in all, the presence of these young men was a welcome addition to the class, though I kept waiting for them to stop showing up. The men kept enrolling only because of word of mouth between these athletes, from one year to the next. In the grand scheme of things, it was a small revolution, but it seemed disproportionately revolutionary to my women students. It meant so much to them that men were showing up to take a class "about them."

This story tells us a lot about how we value people of different genders. Such is the value of a single male body that Anthony changed the entire perception of my class across the campus. He even raised my profile as a professor. What was originally viewed as a course "just for women" (emphasis on the "just") was suddenly a course subscribed to by men—and not just any men, but popular ones, star athletes.

Even the way I recount this story is telling—that I still feel genuine surprise that a man, a powerful athlete, would show up for a course with "women" in the title. That he would take it seriously. That other men showed up and did the same. How notable!

To put it another way: the presence of one masculine body was perceived as worth more than the presence of thirty feminine ones (across two sections). This one man was praised and lauded for his presence by his women peers, for his "courage" to wade into topics men weren't "supposed to" care about. This "courage" to think about women and gender on an intellectual level was contagious among the other men on campus. The men who took the class were also able to defy the wider expectations around masculinity and were praised by the women for being so enlightened.

Of course, the fact that the first man and all the later male students in this class were athletes—popular, star athletes, who were also generally either juniors or seniors—put them in a better position to make such choices. Male athletes are some of the most valuable, powerful, popular people on campus—the most valuable bodies in our midst. And on this campus, a bunch of them chose to use their positions of privilege and power to take a Women and Spirituality class and challenge the prevailing norms around masculinity. Sadly, this isn't the case for male athletes everywhere.

We've Gotten Men Wrong

When I first set out to do research about sex on campus, I assumed that the young men I interviewed would live up to the stereotypes: that they would be callous and vulgar about sex and their partners, that they'd all be in favor of hookup culture and its easy access to sex without commitment, that they would talk about how hookups were the best thing about college. I wasn't completely sure these stereotypes would hold, since the men who showed up in my classes tended to thwart them. But I'd be lying if I said I didn't think those students would prove to be the exception rather than the rule. Boy, was I wrong.

Most young men, behind closed doors and in the safety of a private room, with someone they would never see again (me), tell a different story than we might expect about who they really are and what they want from sex and their partners. One after the other, the young men I interviewed told me something like this: in an ideal world, they would like to be in a long-term romantic relationship, even during college, at least eventually. Many of them would like to find love. I heard the same from women. But the difference lay in what young men felt they were allowed to say publicly.

We expect women to complain about a campus culture that discourages long-term relationships and favors ambivalent, callous, one-time sexual encounters. We expect them to be searching for love and romance. However, we expect something different of men. We assume men will exalt in such a culture and see it as ideally made for them and their insatiable sex drives. We expect them to eschew love and romance for meaningless hookups. Such stereotypes forced the young men I interviewed into an ongoing circle of silence about their desires for relationships. These young men had internalized the notion that to desire love and partnership—and to admit this publicly—was emasculating. It imperiled their status among other guys and even among women.

These stereotypes forced the men to be dishonest about what they said they want in order to protect their social status. They were expected, they felt, to have a series of random sexual conquests and to callously and vulgarly boast about them to friends. Interviewees spoke about how these expectations lessened a bit once they reached junior or senior year, when they could trade in their conquests for a girlfriend. By then, because they'd racked up a long line of hookups, they felt it was OK to settle down into a relationship. But to admit that they wanted a girlfriend from the outset, that they were looking for love, that they might even wish for meaningful sex with a partner during their first year of college? This was regarded as social suicide.

When I talk about this at lectures, men start coming out of the woodwork to discuss it. Maybe not publicly, during the Q&A, but they will line up to talk to me individually afterward, to tell me how they, too, have learned to feel shame about their desires to find love and a relationship during college. They've learned that to not toe this line is to risk their masculinity and their reputation. They usually feel relieved to know they are not alone in feeling so divided between their public and private selves. But they are still unwilling to risk admitting their real feelings in public.

Hookup culture takes the worst traits of stereotypical masculinity—the notion that to be a man is to be impenetrable, made of steel, without feeling or care toward others—and prescribes them for everyone. Very few young men I've spoken with over the last decade recognize themselves and their desires in hookup culture. They don't see it as a culture that is about them or for them. They see themselves as being swept up in the tide of this culture, rather helplessly, just as much as the women I have interviewed. They go along with it, nervous they might be found out to be fraudulent men, men who aren't up to the public performance of masculinity that hookup culture requires of them. This performance of masculinity is more about proving themselves to male peers than it is about sex. But it is also a performance for women, to prove to them that they are normal guys.

Stereotypical masculinity requires boys and young men to alienate themselves from the meaning and benefits of human connection, requiring them to publicly alienate themselves from their private needs and yearnings. By the time men arrive at college, most have spent their entire lives imbibing problematic norms about masculinity, one of which is the notion that all men are sexually insatiable, and another of which is that, while women supposedly get emotional during sex, men do not (or they aren't supposed to). These norms discourage empathy in men, especially in the presence of women sexual partners.

All this performing and posturing teaches young men that manhood means hiding who you really are, hiding your true desires, hiding your emotional and vulnerable sides, and not being yourself in public. It requires performing the disrespect of women and the disrespect of sex.

So what does this mean for sexual assault and consent?

Not All Men Are Perpetrators (But They're Raised to Think They Should Be)

Ever since sexual assault cases have risen to the level of national public scandal, the tension on campus around sex talk—particularly sexual assault talk—has risen to a fever pitch. This is one of the main reasons that lecturing about sex has started to feel like disarming a bomb. Men on campus feel implicated as perpetrators by virtue of the fact that they are men. They worry that women believe that, at night and with enough alcohol, just about any man on campus might turn into a sexual predator.

Of course, while not all college men commit sexual assault, most college sexual assault is committed by men. The sheer statistics around campus sexual violence are staggering: approximately 20 to 25 percent of women experience sexual violence during their college years, and that violence is nearly always perpetrated by their male peers.[1]

However, this does not mean that the numbers of male perpetrators are equally high. Most sexual violence is committed by a small percentage of men who are repeat offenders. But college men feel that everyone is looking at them as the reason we are having a national conversation about sexual assault. The anger, frustration, and shame they feel are palpable. I can't tell you how many questions I've fielded from men about what they see as an unfair bias against them, about their fears of being accused of sexual misconduct and the dire consequences of this, about their worry that men are being denied due process because of Title IX, and about their wish that women not lump them in with men that they, too, find reprehensible. Young men on campus want to hear me affirm in public that they are not all monsters (or potential monsters).

Both research and interviews with young men do affirm just this: the majority of college men are actually sensitive, vulnerable, respectful people who yearn for meaningful social, romantic, and sexual connections just as much as women do (even if they are also struggling to appear casual about these feelings). Michael Kimmel, who has devoted his career to researching boys, men, and masculinity, has found a significant difference between the public performance of masculinity of young men (especially when it relates to groups of men such as fraternities and sports teams on college campuses) and who the men believe themselves to be in private.[2] Yet the public performance of masculinity still tells another story. And while gallons of ink have been spilled about the problems with gender stereotyping of women, similar discussions of men and masculinity are few. The problem is particularly acute among fraternity brothers and athletes, who are more likely to commit sexual transgressions and also more likely to embody this kind of problematic masculinity.

Athletic and fraternity culture, left unchecked, can reinforce the worst stereotypes of men and masculinity for those groups, but also for the rest of the campus, since athletes and powerful fraternity members often set the tone for what it means to be a man. But these men could also use this privilege for good—if we encouraged them to do so. A number of universities and several scholars (Michael Kimmel, again, is one prominent example) are encouraging men to take the lead in sexual assault prevention and bystander education, empowering men to step up and speak out about this issue, becoming role models as opposed to symbols of the perpetrator as men on campus are so often labeled. The work of professors like Kimmel and educators like Jackson Katz, who are actively challenging stereotypical conceptions of men and masculinity in the classroom and on campus overall, is particularly promising—and it is essential work, if we hope to change things not just for women but for men, too.[3]

The masculinity of men at the top of the food chain—the star athletes, the leaders of the fraternities, the most attractive and popular men on campus—is likely more secure than that of many (maybe even most) of their male peers. These are the enviable men on campus, who don't have to work as hard to establish themselves as "real men" because people automatically regard them as such. They are in the best position to thwart problematic stereotypes of masculinity, to critique them, to correct peers who display the worst (and, yes, the criminal) traits of male aggression. These are also the men who are in a position to empower male peers on campus to express positive traits like emotional openness and accessibility, investment in relationships, and vulnerability. They can show their male peers that it's okay to be vulnerable, emotional, and caring, that it's actually unmanly to act otherwise. They are in a position to help transform the campus climate, yet we've done little to harness their power for good, to empower and encourage these men to use their status to shift the conversation about men in a different, more powerful direction. Given the vastly negative reputations of fraternities and athletic teams, one would think it would be in everyone's interests to teach these men to use their power in different ways—if only to improve their organizations' and teams' reputations.

The Ways We Fail Boys and Young Men

The cost of all this is enormous. We uncritically socialize boys and men to be aggressors: on the playing field, in the workplace, in the bedroom. To be a man is to assert one's power and superiority over others, especially women (more on this kind of othering in the next chapter). To be a man—especially a white man—is to be entitled.

Until recently, the workplace and the classroom have been spheres for men, of men, about men. While I may not agree with Hanna Rosin in her assessment of hookup culture, her arguments in *The End of Men* about the ways women are taking over the workplace and occupying powerful positions that come with it are spot on. Now that powerful men are being held accountable for sexual harassment and assault in the entertainment industry and the media, the workplace will experience even greater changes in the coming years. The same goes for the classroom and the university. Women now constitute, on average, approximately 55 percent of the college student body (the number keeps going up), and they are often running away with most of the academic awards to boot. The new prominence of Title IX as a tool to force universities to address sexual harassment and assault across not only its student body but also its staff, administration, and faculty is shifting the balance of power between men and women on campus.

Yet boys and men are still raised to believe that power and acclaim are their birthright. When women are successful in spheres that have traditionally been considered a man's world, men can interpret this as women "taking away" what is rightfully theirs. One of the ways that men can lash out and have lashed out in the past, expressing anger and dismay at their loss of power in these spheres, is through sexual aggression. Only recently are we, as a society, beginning to hold them accountable for this behavior.

We need to teach boys and young men to develop the self-awareness necessary to change these behaviors. The fact that our cultural and academic conversations around men and masculinity are lacking means that boys and men likely don't have access to a critique of the power structures in which they are enmeshed.

They play out their prescribed roles, typically with little critical reflection and self-awareness that they are doing this. Few young men have the opportunity to critique the norms of masculinity. The price of this lack of self-awareness can be steep. The angry, dismayed, and worried men sitting in the audience at my lectures know this, and their sense of sudden powerlessness—of the loss of power—is part of what's fueling resistance to Title IX. The cultural norms around masculinity that reify aggression (especially aggression toward women) are the same norms that can lead to sexual violence. Men on campus are caught in a problematic web of conflicting expectations, yet we've done little to talk to them about this openly and honestly, and yes, with some sensitivity to their predicament.

Not all men are perpetrators, but we've socialized them to think they're supposed to exhibit voracious sexual aggression. But just as the norms and values of a culture of hooking up are at odds with consent, so stereotypical masculinity is at odds with a culture of consent. For a young man to risk going against masculine norms and scripts can also be to risk his place in the social schema of a campus. When men speak up angrily about how the conversation around sexual violence isn't fair to them, they have a point. It isn't fair that they've grown up in a culture that teaches them one thing and then expects them to be something else. It's confusing to be asked to navigate competing cultural claims and expectations, risking one's social status in the process, without adequate discussion.

Colleges and universities should be places where men go to unpack these stereotypes, where they are challenged to critique the societal structures and values that shape masculinity and their own views of what it means to be a man. We should be having these kinds of conversations at every college in this country. Yet we aren't—at least not yet. There are courses popping up around the country dedicated to studying masculinity, but they are still too few and far between.[4] We need to offer young people of all genders an intellectually rigorous space dedicated to the investigation of men and masculinity. Doing so is one step toward transforming the role that stereotypical ideas of masculinity play in the culture of assault and harassment on our campuses.

6 | A HIERARCHY OF BODIES
SEXUAL PRIVILEGE, GENDER,
SHAME, AND BLAME

The Most Vulnerable of Bodies

Men, white men, occupy a privileged place in our culture. And that privilege is not merely conceptual—it's physical. Male bodies occupy positions of disproportionate power in the workplace, on our campuses, in our classrooms, and in the bedroom, too. In our society, certain bodies are treated as more valuable than others. Bodies are organized vertically, with particular kinds of bodies residing on the lower rungs, while others rest comfortably along the top. White bodies are more valuable than black ones. Rich bodies are more valuable than poor ones. Healthy bodies more than disabled bodies. Thin bodies more than fat bodies. Beautiful bodies more than ugly bodies. Heterosexual bodies more than homosexual ones. Any body more than transgender bodies.

We tell ourselves all kinds of stories to justify our biases, to rationalize why it is OK to walk by a homeless body, why we are powerless to change things for this particular body, why it's all right for us to ignore the suffering and loneliness that we face regularly on the streets. We internalize notions of "good bodies" and "bad bodies" according to preconceived ideas about race, ethnicity, gender, and many other factors, and we treat the new bodies we encounter according to those criteria, often without realizing we are doing so. Our reactions to different bodies are based on cultural biases and scripts we've imbibed over the course of our lifetimes and perform without thinking. We see some bodies as criminal without knowing anything about them, fearing and avoiding those bodies. We demonize certain bodies as "unnatural." Likewise, we assume that other bodies are upstanding citizens, without knowing anything about those people either, and act accordingly, treating them differently, as worthy of respect.

We worship certain bodies, too—especially on campus. We worship the tall, beautiful blonde in the most prestigious sorority, as she flicks her hair while walking across the campus green. We worship the star quarterback on the football team, cheering for him, screaming ourselves hoarse. We smile, shake the football players' hands, lavish them with praise, ask for their autographs. And the students who are worshipped bask in their status. For anyone who is a student or who works or teaches on a college campus, you likely already know who these students are, the ones at the very top of the social hierarchy. People defer to them, wish they could be them, and treat them accordingly. We (often unknowingly) reinforce this hierarchy of bodies at our own colleges.

On all campuses, there is a hierarchy of bodies as well as an unwritten code and formula for determining that hierarchy. On campuses with Greek life, this code is more public and more officially ratified by the university administration than at schools without it. These campuses quite literally celebrate nearly all-white sororities and fraternities that legislate according to beauty, wealth, accomplishment, and even hair color. (Just take a look at the University of Alabama sorority recruitment video that went viral in 2015 as an example, really a caricature, of this. In the "Alabama Alpha Phi 2015" video, sorority women, nearly all of them white, dressed in white, with long blond hair, blow kisses, throw glitter, and jump and dance in string bikinis.)[1]

Sororities and fraternities systematize and publicize which bodies they deem most valuable and desirable and actively recruit those bodies in the effort to maintain their pristine image. Discriminating between bodies, deeming some bodies as undesirable, as worthy only of mocking and humiliating, or not even worth acknowledging at all, becomes the purview. The societies must be kept pure, and purity requires careful cultivation of who is allowed in and who must be excluded at all costs.

Athletes, too, are the beneficiaries of a university-supported system of entitlement that values and protects their bodies more than others. Universities, alumni, trustees, local residents, and even local police departments can become invested in certain athletes and teams because of the school's reputation as an athletic powerhouse and because athletes and teams can be huge moneymakers. They form layers of protection around (almost always male) players. Sometimes, the protection is for academic misconduct, but other times, higher-ups at universities will look the other way when athletes commit felonies, or they may even collude in covering up these crimes. The message sent by these actions to the collective student body is that male athletic bodies are so important, so valuable, so essential, that they are entitled to do whatever they want. They are above recrimination.

And that extends to sexual assault. Though they would never state it this way, when coaches, administrators, alumni, and others cover up sexual crimes by athletes, they are showing that athletes have the right to have sex with any woman they want, to force women to have sex, or to simply have sex with their passed-out bodies in full-on gang rapes, because all other bodies on campus, especially female bodies, rank below theirs in the hierarchy. Women's bodies are there for the taking. And because athletic bodies can be worth millions in revenue, it isn't difficult to do the math and figure out which bodies the university will value.

This hierarchy of bodies is intimately linked to the pervasive problem of sexual violence and our failure to deal with it. Sexual violence is considered a "women's issue," and therefore it gets pushed to the bottom of an institution's priorities.

One of the most sickening moments in the documentary *The Hunting Ground* is a simple listing of campus reports of sexual assault by women that were ignored, swept under the rug, or mishandled because the reports were made against star athletes.[2] This list exposes the pattern of such incidents at universities across the country. *The New York Times* ran a lengthy exposé about Florida State Heisman Trophy winner Jameis Winston, who faced a rape allegation. The university and the police conspired to ensure Winston would not be charged.[3] Reports and similar scandals around star athletes and star teams at universities all over the United States could fill the entirety of this book.

In our culture, a single man's body can be deemed so valuable that it warrants the covering up of rapes. This hierarchy we perpetuate is one of the dominant operating scripts that certain men inherit and use to perpetuate and hide sexual violence. And we can't put an end to sexual violence on campus unless we dismantle this hierarchy.

Gendered Norms around Violence: The Shame of It

Why is it that universities have taken up the issue of sexual violence only recently even though the number of sexual assaults has held steady for decades? It's not as though schools have been unaware that sexual violence is a problem. But only since the federal government began interpreting Title IX as requiring universities to take sexual assault seriously—and accompanied this requirement with the threat of investigations and losing government funding—have universities finally started paying attention.

These situations should provoke us to wonder why. Why does it take threats and public scandal for universities to address sexual violence? Why is something that is such a pervasive problem—with one-fifth to one quarter of women experiencing it during their time on campus—not significant enough to address on its own without pressure from the federal government? (And what happens now, if Betsy DeVos turns a blind eye to the issue?) What does this mean for our views of women? For the valuing (and devaluing) of women's bodies?

Perhaps this means that colleges and universities respond only to threats. Sexual assault has long been considered a women's issue, plain and simple, and therefore of lesser importance than other issues. Women overall offer an institution less value. Women athletes don't bring in big revenues. When the number of women on campus grows, and more women achieve academic successes and awards, people get worried, concerned that the school will lose some of its desirability. People begin to cry out how this is unfair to boys—we need to help the men catch up. Women's success makes people nervous and uncomfortable. Men's success is normal. It's the way things are supposed to be.

Sexual violence is diminished and devalued on our campuses in the same way that all women's issues are devalued in the hierarchies of power embedded in our institutions. Women and girls are less important, less worthy. Our bodies are lower in the hierarchy and therefore more disposable, and thus they are easier to ignore when they are violated. Women and girls are physically weaker, so it is understandable that the site of sexual assault is the feminine or feminized body. Women's bodies are sites for punishment, places for men to enact their rage, their power-over, to reassure themselves that their bodies are stronger than women's. This narrative of masculinity and men asserting their rights and power over women is affirmed and reaffirmed on a campus even when down the hall professors and students are engaged in the act of critiquing it.

Part of the problem is that we don't have enough professors and students engaged in this critique, and part of why we don't is because the institutions themselves diminish and devalue those individuals on campus who do engage in this critique (more on this later). Ask any gender studies professor about this, and you'll get an earful. Feminists of all stripes have been discussing sexual assault for decades, but we do so within institutions that diminish feminism and feminists. There are too few of us in number to take on such a systemic problem.

Much ink has been spilled in discussing the fears that girls and women experience their entire lives about sexual violence, the fears of walking down the street, walking across a parking lot, getting into one's car at night, walking home from a party late and alone. I don't know exactly when I learned this myself, at what point it became clear that to be in a woman's body meant that the possibility of rape was always just around the corner. But somehow this knowledge seeped in as I grew up, and eventually it became as normal and as much a part of life as putting on shoes before going out the door in the morning. It's no wonder college women bristle when told not to walk alone at night, when advised to always travel in groups of friends. Women long to find truly safe spaces, but in reality nowhere is safe—or, at least, nowhere *feels* safe—not even the campus quad, not even among one's peers or at parties.

Facing this reality can be devastating. But it is also, frankly, exhausting, maddening, and enraging.

Even worse, our culture uses this reality and these fears to blame women when they are assaulted. We tell women that they should have known better than to walk alone at night, that they should have known better than to go down that street, that they should have known better than to go to a party at that fraternity that is widely known on campus for being a place to get raped. Women learn as we grow up to feel responsible for what happens to us, for drawing negative attention to ourselves with our bodies, with the way we dress, with the places we go. These ideas seep into us to our very cores, and we internalize an acute sense that it is our own fault if someone else chooses to violate our bodies and our lives.

Just as gender is culturally constructed, just as masculinity is scripted and narrated through a set of inherited norms, so sexual violence is feminized in the narratives and scripts we inherit about women and women's bodies in our culture and on our campuses. To be the object of sexual violence is to be disempowered and overpowered on a bodily level, which is to say, to be proved weak in body, to be unable to protect one's body from harm, to be unable to fend off another's body. And just as anything associated with women is less valued, sexual violence, as a women's issue, is regarded as less of a crisis.

That is, until the government threatens a campus, making it sit up and take notice. Or until men with tremendous power and public prestige in our culture have suffered reprimand, censure, and the loss of their jobs and careers because they are finally being held accountable for past instances of assault and harassment.

Name-Calling and the Objectification of Bodies

In " 'Good Girls': Gender, Social Class, and Slut Discourse on Campus," Elizabeth A. Armstrong and colleagues speak of a pervasive fear among college women, even the most privileged among them, of being labeled a "slut." It is a label that is tied not only to gender but also to class and privilege. "High-status women employ slut discourse to assert class advantage, defining themselves as classy rather than trashy, while low-status women express class resentment—deriding rich, bitchy sluts for their exclusivity," Armstrong and her colleagues write. "Slut discourse enables, rather than constrains, sexual experimentation for the high-status women whose definitions prevail in the dominant social scene. This is a form of sexual privilege. In contrast, low-status women risk public shaming when they attempt to enter dominant social worlds."[4] All women, including high-status women, are afraid of attracting the label of "slut," but high-status women strive to get the upper hand in this discourse, doing their best to control who gets the label.[5] Just as there is a hierarchy of bodies ordered according to gender, race, sexual orientation, and economic background, there is also a hierarchy within each gender, a kind of "sexual privilege" that is enjoyed.[6]

When I did my initial research about sex on campus, this kind of name-calling was rampant—mainly among the young women I interviewed, though it was certainly present among the men as well. It was from men that I learned the term "dirty girl," which refers to someone who should be avoided because she is known to have hooked up with lots of people and is thought likely to have sexually transmitted diseases.[7] When I asked the first young man who told me about "dirty girls" whether men ever get labeled as "dirty," he laughed and told me no. Apparently, men who hook up with lots of partners are immune to negative labels and also immune to sexually transmitted infections. In fact, men who hook up with lots of women are celebrated as "players," who are understood as men who should be respected for their many conquests. Yet any woman who engages in similar behavior is under threat—and she knows it, all women know it—of being called a slut.

References to hos and sluts came up often in my interviews with women and men in their discussion of theme parties on campus, the most popular among them being "Pimps and Hos," "CEO's and Office Hos," "Politicians and Prostitutes," "Football Stars and Cheerleader Sluts," and "Millionaires and Maids."[8] These themes, taken straight from porn, follow traditional patriarchal binaries and scripts about men in positions of power and dominance, including sexual power and dominance, with women always relegated to the subservient, submissive, and sexually available positions.[9] In a college culture where women themselves are supposedly aspiring CEOs, athletic stars, and politicians, that the role of women at a party is still to be sexually available to men who occupy positions of power—at least men who are performing these positions of power at a party—shows exactly how women's bodies continue to be devalued not only in our culture but also on our campuses, where, again, entire departments may be devoted to critiquing exactly these sorts of scripts and patriarchal structures.

The devaluing of a woman's body is, quite literally, on full display at a theme party whose entire point is that the woman's body is laid bare for the pleasure and the taking of the men. The role of the man is to celebrate this and to do his best to take full advantage of so many scantily clad, supposedly sexually available women in attendance. To assert his sexual privilege over a woman's body, to exploit her body because that is a man's right in the accepted hierarchy. In these sorts of scenarios, the goal is to turn the woman's body (especially) into an object for sexual use.

"Part of the social context of women's lives in the United States is the experience of being treated as a sexual object, or as a body that exists for the pleasure of others," write Melanie Hill and Ann Fischer in their article "Examining Objectification Theory."[10] It is considered normal and natural to objectify the bodies of women and girls, far more so than the bodies of men. Indeed, women and girls objectify each other's bodies, and both men and women engage in the slut shaming of women as well as the abuse of women's bodies. According to Hill and Fischer, "Women may be socialized not only to see themselves as objects but perhaps to see other women as objects as well. In other words, since both men and women are socialized in a culture that sexually objectifies women, both men and women may come to internalize this socialization and sexually objectify women. Women come to experience not only themselves, but other women as well, through the 'eyes of the indeterminate observer.' "[11]

Objects, things, and toys are inanimate, inhuman, designed to be used for specific functions, as means to an end. Objects can be broken, abused, damaged, and then thrown in the trash because they are disposable, and new ones can always be acquired. Hookup culture on campus exacerbates the scripts men and women inherit about objectification. The endgame of hookup culture is to act on the belief that bodies are sexual objects. In this context, bodies are not ends in and of themselves; they are a means toward orgasm. The purpose of one's partner's body in a hookup is to take advantage of that body sexually. "The common thread running through all forms of sexual objectification," write scholars Barbara Fredrickson and Tomi-Ann Roberts, "is the experience of being treated *as a body* (or collection of body parts) valued predominantly for its use to (or consumption by) others." Objectification occurs when the body or body parts and functions are "reduced to the status of mere instruments."[12]

Taken to the extreme, we are socialized to understand that the passed-out body of a college woman is the ideal sexual object. She is unable to talk, to move on her own, and certainly she is unable to say no. She becomes like a plastic sex toy, except infinitely better because she is not actually plastic. She is ready to be used and abused and played with by one or more male parties.

She becomes the "mere instrument" for the pleasure of the rapist, the body to be "used" and "consumed." Situations such as the ones in Steubenville (where a passed out young woman was repeatedly sexually assaulted by her peers, including several members of Steubenville's storied high school football team) and at Stanford occur because these norms exist and persist. This is how a man or group of men come to believe they are entitled to use an inert body however they choose.

The pervasive and continued sexual objectification of women on our college campuses forces women to live with the societal reality of violence against their bodies. They must learn to cope with constant anxiety about it. They are forced to employ strategies of self-defense, awareness of surroundings, and decision-making around personal safety on a constant basis. These are the kinds of "rape prevention" tactics that universities frame as consent education. But women are tired of serving as the primary defense against sexual violence on campus. Which brings us to the issue of victim blaming.

A Devil's Bargain: Victim Blaming

Victim blaming is the act of declaring a person who is making accusations of sexual assault to be responsible for their own assault. By blaming women for instances of sexual violence, and creating a prohibitive, threatening environment for making accusations of assault, we establish an environment in which most victims will opt not to report sexual violence. Examples of victim blaming include interrogating victims about their decision-making during sex, their dress, their level of alcohol consumption, and their self-awareness about risky situations and judging them about any other number of things they might have done to prevent or avoid being assaulted. Asking questions like, "Are you *sure* you didn't want to?" or "Do you think there's anything you could have done differently?" or "Did you really think you could pass out and nothing would happen?" puts the accuser on the defensive and makes the person feel as though what happened is at least partially if not entirely her fault. Holding up the alleged perpetrator as someone who could not possibly have done such a thing is another way of disempowering someone's claim to having been assaulted.

Worse still, slut shaming can exacerbate victim blaming, since "slutty women" are always "asking for it"—or so the thinking goes. Women who have been labeled sluts have a more difficult time convincing others that they were raped. The kind of sexual privilege Hamilton and Armstrong describe as having class components applies here. Women who are not deemed "classy"—those who are nonwhite, economically disadvantaged, or not attractive according to campus norms—will face more difficulty getting others to believe their accusations. A "classy," sexually privileged women might not face as much attack—though she'll likely still face some.

All women, even the most sexually privileged, are vulnerable to labels and victim blaming, especially if they accuse someone who is perceived to be above them in the hierarchy.[13] Even the most powerful sorority woman will face the same hurdles as other women if she is assaulted by an even more powerful—and therefore more valuable—man on campus. The sorority woman may feel even greater pressure to remain silent about an assault, so as not to upset the status quo within the Greek system and bring negative attention to the sorority.

The potential to be victim-blamed will silence accusations of sexual violence before they are even made. As noted earlier, surveys have found that upward of 80 percent of victims on college campuses do not report their assaults—and it's no wonder.[14] Colleges are known to employ lawyers who use victim-blaming tactics to defend their clients when a university's response to an accusation is questioned, or when a university's championship-level athletic program is "threatened."[15] As with slut shaming, victim blaming can escalate or diminish based on the status and privilege of both the accuser and the accused. If the accused is the star quarterback on campus, not only does the potential for victim blaming skyrocket, but it becomes ever more frightening for the accuser to come forward. Women are caught in a devil's bargain: decide to remain silent about an assault, burying it, for fear of retribution, or tell someone and face the wrath of the public and their peers, with more shame and humiliation piled on top.[16]

In 2016, Erica Kinsman, who grew up in the shadow of Florida State, eventually won a historic settlement against FSU because of its mishandling of her case against football star Jameis Winston. But it was a long, terrible road to get there. In *The Hunting Ground*, Kinsman explains that when she reported her assault to the police, and the officer realized who she was accusing, she was told by the investigator, "This is a huge football town, you really should think long and hard about whether you want to press charges or not." In response to Kinsman's claim, the police did absolutely nothing for ten months. At the time of Kinsman's accusation, Winston was on track not only to win the Heisman Trophy but to lead FSU to a national football championship. When news of her accusation broke, male sportscasters like Skip Bayless and Stephen A. Smith expressed their sympathy for Winston on-air at ESPN and their outrage that Kinsman would try to tarnish his reputation.[17] Kinsman was harassed, called a slut and a whore. She received threats, as did her family and her sorority (people threatened to burn it down). Kinsman dropped out of FSU as a result.[18]

All too often, because a university culture has become so hostile to someone's claim of assault, the accuser can no longer bear to remain on campus.[19] In the most tragic and extreme of circumstances, some students have resorted to suicide. Lizzy Seeberg, a first-year student at Saint Mary's College in South Bend, Indiana, took her own life ten days after reporting to police that she was sexually assaulted by a football player at Notre Dame.[20] The hostility toward rape victims, especially college rape victims, is so widespread that victims whose cases garner national attention (often because of who they are accusing) face yet another level of threats and blame from the wider public. Annie Clark and Andrea Pino, the two young women at the center of *The Hunting Ground*, regularly receive death and rape threats for the ways they have become the public faces of Title IX in relation to campus sexual assault, and for helping other women use the law to hold their universities accountable when the schools have been negligent in the face of allegations.[21]

To call someone a demeaning name, to attach a negative label, is a strategy for gaining power over that person, to diminish their value. Name-calling can silence, alienate, and cripple a person—not only one's reputation but also one's self-esteem. Name-calling and victim blaming reinforce the hierarchy of bodies, making it easier to look the other way when sexual violence occurs.

When young college men who have been accused of rape are actually held accountable in court, the public often seems more worried about their fates, about their promising lives and careers suddenly ruined, than about the victims. The judge in the Brock Turner case certainly worried a great deal about Turner's future (provoking a firestorm of anger in response). He seemed more concerned about Turner than about the young woman Turner brutally raped behind a dumpster. When faced with perpetrators of sexual violence on campus—almost always young men on their way to great things—we hem and haw about what these young men might lose. But we don't seem quite as worried about the futures ruined, the careers and educations cut short among the women victims of sexual violence. We'd rather they just shut up and keep it to themselves, not make such a fuss, just learn to live with it and move on.

And we should worry about these young men—because they are so young, because they are also our children and our students, because it will indeed change their lives if they are held accountable for sexual violence. But we should worry *why* they committed such violence. We should wonder how we can stop other young men in our lives from becoming perpetrators of sexual violence, too.

And we need to worry a great deal more about the young women that these young men have victimized.

Why don't we become more outraged on behalf of our young women victims? What does this say about the power (and powerlessness), the value (and devaluing) of women on our campuses and in our wider society? Why do we, as a culture, feel more sympathy for young male perpetrators of sexual violence than for young women victims of it? Why is it we are so resistant to diving into the work required to change our communities with regard to sexual violence? Why will we invest so much money in new football stadiums and residence hall renovations but not in the resources necessary to deal with the sexual violence that affects somewhere between 20 and 25 percent of our student populations of women?

It's no wonder that women will choose silence over reporting an assault, when doing so means facing so many people who will shake their heads at you and wish you would would just go away.

Women Are Socialized to Blame and to Doubt

There is yet another type of shame and blame that disempowers women: the shame and blame we learn to direct at ourselves. Girls and women are socialized to monitor their own behavior and be aware of how it might invite the wrong kind of attention.[22]

After the revelation of Donald Trump's boasting about behavior that could be construed as sexual assault, the writer Kelly Hall started a movement on Twitter, asking women to tweet their "first assaults." Hall soon received an onslaught of stories from all over the world, examples of harassment and assault that ranged from unwanted looks and kisses to violent stranger rape. Notable among the themes that emerged from this Twitter blitz was the undercurrent of self-blame that women expressed about so many of these encounters, and how their attempts to brush off their experiences as supposedly too "small" about which to be upset caused them to suffer in silence. In an article in the the *New York Times* about this impromptu Twitter movement, reporter Jonathan Mahler picked out one particular tweet that speaks directly to the ways that women learn from an early age to blame themselves for the sins of others. "Grabbed from behind on the street," begins the tweet from Lynne Boschee, now fifty. "Thought it was my fault because I was wearing a dress. Never told anyone. I was 14."[23]

In an opinion piece titled "What Does a Lifetime of Leers Do to Us?," Jessica Valenti writes about the everyday objectification of women, of catcalls on the street, of unwanted advances, of subway assaults, of how simply living "while female" not only shapes us but also can inure us to the near-constant sexist treatment that women face every day.[24]

In our culture, tragically, we raise girls and women to believe that their identity rests on the ability to attract male attention of all kinds, even the "negative," leering kind, yet that somehow, in performing our femininity this way, we are also responsible for warding off whatever a man might do once we have attracted his attention—that is, harass, assault, or rape us. We are also responsible for brushing off harassment and even assault as "normal" or as what Donald Trump has discounted as mere "locker room talk," the kind of "boys will be boys" behavior that people have used for far too long to excuse vulgar, demeaning, and violent behavior and attitudes toward women.

Women on campus and beyond feel righteous outrage at the fact that the focus is still on women doing the preventing, rather than on preventing rapists from raping, or on the cultural norms that perpetuate rape culture. We shame and blame women and let men off the hook. We've known for decades that sexual violence is a major problem on campus, but we do little about it—until the government forces us to. And now that colleges and universities are being forced to do something, conservatives have come out to denounce their actions as criminalizing masculinity.

This reality provokes a number of questions: How do we tackle so many biases, so many problematic scripts about masculinity and femininity, about sex and hooking up, about who is more valuable than whom and why? How do we transform a campus culture (and a wider culture) that has shrugged its shoulders at pervasive sexual violence for decades? And how do we do it within schools that have institutionalized the degradation and diminishment of this work and the individuals on campus who do it? We certainly don't do it with one-hour educational events during first-year orientations or with university lawyers. The task at hand may seem mountainous, even too mountainous to tackle.

But just as the scripts and narratives that help perpetuate sexual violence are embedded in our campuses, the stories we need to transform universities and colleges into communities that foster a culture of consent are, too. All the tools we need are right there for us. We just need to decide to use them—and to reframe some of the structures and values of our institutions to draw them out, give them support, and make them priorities.

PART III

Telling the Story of Consent

REWRITING AND TRANSFORMING
CAMPUS NARRATIVES

7 | WHEN CULTURE AND SEXUAL ETHICS ARE GOOD

PREPARING OURSELVES TO DO NECESSARY WORK

First: Setting Aside Cynicism about Culture

I've spent a lot of time describing the negative effects of campus culture. But culture is necessary. In the best of circumstances, it helps us to be better versions of ourselves and to build healthier communities. It provides us with narratives that empower and liberate, that inspire, that help us discover our gifts and talents and find a way to use and celebrate them. It connects us to others. It doesn't alienate, oppress, and repress us. It honors our humanity and our diversity.

Maybe it sounds like I'm describing a utopia. Maybe, in a way, I am.

But aren't universities supposed to be utopian places? The places where we strive for such possibilities? Beacons of hope and light and opportunity, at least in theory? There's nothing wrong with hanging on to this dream. The only thing stopping us from doing so is cynicism. To address sexual violence, to truly address it, we must set our cynicism aside because it won't be useful—certainly not to the project of building a culture of consent.

We are at a crossroads in higher education because of the sexual assault crisis. Ideas about how we do things are being upended, throwing schools into turmoil. This doesn't have to be a bad thing. Upending the status quo can provide an opportunity to restructure our institutions and communities in new, better, and more empowering ways, to create systemic goods as opposed to systemic ills. At the very least, we need to try.

Second: Consent Is a Way of Being

In 2015, a video called "Tea Consent" went viral. It's a short, funny cartoon demonstrating how to understand sexual consent through an analogy of offering someone a cup of tea. It's basically a consent-for-dummies educational video whose purpose is to illustrate that consent is easy—easy to understand, perform, and respect. A little under three minutes and you're done! Consent understood. Necessary education over.

In some ways, understanding consent *is* easy.

It *does* seem simple—as simple as yes or no.

But we are making consent deceptively simple, because to claim that it is easy is to ignore rape culture; to ignore biases and stereotypes about femininity and masculinity; to ignore the ambivalence that pervades hookup culture; to ignore the confusion, awkwardness, insecurity, and anxiety that so many people have about sex; to ignore the complexity of human desire, of human vulnerability, of human relationship. The list could go on. The university is a place built to tackle complexity, one where we should be able to examine who we are as people who live in community with others, and whose communities are infected with insidious strains of sexual violence.

We must get beyond consent as mere words, acknowledging that prioritizing consent is also prioritizing a set of ethics. We must acknowledge that consent isn't just about sex—it is a way of *being toward others*. By creating a set of ethical expectations and values that reflect this, we can create a culture of consent.

Third: Getting Comfortable with Being Ethical (While Having Sex)

Talking about ethics, sexual ethics in particular, makes my students nervous, uncomfortable, and resistant. This is because they associate sexual ethics with a series of "don'ts" that they were told about sex while growing up, often in the context of a religious tradition. The Catholic students I interviewed for my study about sex on campus rolled their eyes and huffed about how all they learned from Catholicism about sex were what I came to think of as the "three don'ts of sex" if you're Catholic: don't do it, don't use condoms, and don't be gay. Students felt these commandments not only were entirely negative, prohibitive, and discriminatory but also were useless to anyone attending college, especially a college where the norms of hookup culture dominate. These students have become allergic to sexual ethics.

Liberals, too, have developed similar allergies. I know, because I am one. Sexual ethics scares many of us, even repels and repulses us, because when we enter into the realm of sexual ethics, we are once again stepping onto one of our society's fiercest partisan battlefields. We are talking about "values," and we shudder in the face of the word. We get worried about one-size-fits-all anything, especially when we are talking about sexual ethics (even as many of us fail to acknowledge the way that hookup culture is also one-size-fits-all). After all, the people who talk most openly and forcefully about values are conservative Christians ("values voters"), many of whom promote a sexual ethic that does exactly what so many of my students rail about: forbid premarital sex, oppose gay relationships, seek to limit and erase reproductive rights. Needless to say, this is not a sexual ethic that most feminists would want to be associated with.[1]

As communities and as a culture, we've become afraid of attaching meaning to sex. One of the driving questions for this generation, for the mainstream college campus, is whether we can create a culture of consent without giving up the sexual freedoms we've earned over the last half-century, and without capitulating to restrictive, repressive, and patriarchal norms around sex. Can we create an ethics of sex and sexuality, essential in order for a culture of consent to exist, while still hanging on to sexual freedom, respecting sexual diversity, and honoring sexual desires that fall outside societal, religious, and cultural norms? Can consent, sexual freedom, and ethics all coexist, or are they somehow antithetical?

Fears of having to trade one thing for another—consent for freedom, freedom for ethics—have led us to avoid thinking through the mainstream cultural and societal sexual mores (or lack thereof) we are passing along to the next generation. But to simply secede from the conversation about values and ethics is shortsighted. Washing our hands of sexual ethics because we are uncomfortable talking about values leaves young people to fend for themselves. This not only is irresponsible but also goes against everything that advocates of consent are advocating for. If only religious conservatives are talking about values, then the argument about values is ceded to religious conservatives, and they retain all the power. The proper response is not to recuse ourselves from that conversation but to argue for a framework for sexual ethics that helps us arrive at an alternative set of values—values that fit the university communities we would like to build and that reduce sexual violence on our campuses.

When I speak with students about my research, I often ask them to raise their hands if they care about social justice. Everyone inevitably does. Then I ask the students if they care about human dignity. Again, it's unanimous. Then I ask them another set of questions: So where is the human dignity at the parties they go to on the weekends? Where is the attention to social justice there? What about when you are drinking? Hooking up? How do you apply these concerns to your friends and your partners? Do you? And if you don't, why not? Why is it that we, as communities, tend to think of ourselves as exporters of dignity and justice—across the street to the soup kitchen where we (our fraternities and sororities included) volunteer, or somewhere else far away, where we go to build houses and fix water systems? Why do we so fervently practice our concern for dignity and justice elsewhere but not in our own communities, the places where we live among our peers, our friends, our partners? And why is it that we have learned that being ethical while having sex is such a drag? Especially when we care so much about being ethical people?

These questions strike at core concerns among students, who care deeply about who they are and how they act in relation to others. The most important resources we have for establishing a baseline of sexual ethics for our college communities are the broader ethical interests, commitments, and identities of the students themselves. College students see themselves as ethical people. They care about justice and the dignity of all persons, they care about human rights and freedoms. Students may not like to be judged or to feel judged, but they do search for tools and frameworks to help them make good decisions about all sorts of things, including relationships, friendships, and sex, how they party, and even how they drink.

At the moment, on our campuses, discussing "yes" and "no" is usually about as far as we get in teaching sexual ethics. It is an inch-deep conversation in a place where conversations need to get much deeper. Consent must go to the core of who we are as people and how we treat each other. The very values that students indicate they care about must be brought to bear in relation to sex and how we treat our partners. Consent asks us to care about another person in one of the most intimate and vulnerable situations in which we will ever find ourselves, and it asks the same of our partners. It forces us to reckon with the reality and the worth of the human body, to acknowledge its simultaneous fragility and strength, that it can be at once a site of pleasure and joy but also pain and brokenness.

The ethical implications of consent cut straight to the heart of who we are as communities—or at least they should. Sex and sexual ethics are not simply private, individual matters, and neither is consent—we are kidding ourselves if we convince ourselves of this, and we are failing our students in the process. If such matters were truly private, we wouldn't end up with so much public scandal. Consent, our policies around it, and the fact that we are teaching it, or trying to, turns sex into a communal priority and a communal value. The prioritizing of consent on campus is a way of communicating to our students that sexual intimacy—even if it is conducted in private—is of communal concern. Our community standard says that it must be nonviolent and must involve active participation of both parties. As *communities*, we are deciding this. As *communities*, we are setting an ethical standard for sex.

We are doing this already, even if we don't realize it. We are teaching the ethical practice of consent without thinking through the common theoretical grounding from which that practice arises— because we haven't yet acknowledged that we have a sexual ethic. We are cobbling together educational initiatives without doing the difficult and complicated work of addressing what I believe is one of the most significant questions of our time: What does sexual ethics look like in a postreligious society? For those who fear and resist wading into the waters of sexual ethics, who still resist the notion that, by privileging consent, we are advocating a particular vision of sexual ethics—it's time to get over those fears and that resistance.

Consent is an ethical concern, and there is no way around this. It is an ethical act between two partners. Let's stop being in denial and get comfortable with that idea.

Fourth: A Culture of Consent's Implied Framework for Sexual Ethics

I mentioned earlier that we need to argue for an alternative set of values that fit the university communities that we would like to build, and that banish sexual violence from our campuses. I think we already are arguing for a particular sexual ethical framework—indeed, we are requiring community compliance with it. But we are not admitting this openly. Universities are advocating for consent as an essential, required value among all people on our campuses. We put it in the student handbook, and students can be expelled for violating that standard. So it is not as though we are just suggesting consent as a value. We are legislating it as part of the contract everyone agrees to when they walk onto campus. So let's admit this openly and figure out what sort of sexual ethics we are arguing for.

I am going to take a stab at it here—to at least start the conversation.

When we advocate for consent, we are not merely advocating that people say yes or no to sex—that's too simplistic, and everyone knows that sex and sexual decision-making are far more complicated than this, for numerous reasons, including the many scripts and narratives I've critiqued thus far in this book. Consent's underpinnings, its foundations, imply the following ethical expectations for each member of a university community:

Attention, Care, and Regard for the Physical and Emotional Well-Being of One's Partner. To gauge consent, to figure out if one's partner wants to be there or not, requires actually paying attention to how that person is feeling, both physically and emotionally. Does the other person want to be there? Is she or he OK? If not, why not? Turning one's back on one's partner—however metaphorically—risks losing sight of the attention, care, and regard that are necessary to make sure she or he is not upset, unhappy, in physical pain or distress, or wanting to stop. Sex is attentive, in other words, and that attention is ongoing. Sex requires a basic level of regard, attention, and care for one's partner. This is what we are implicitly teaching our students and our community about sex when we advocate for consent.

Sex Is Openly Communicative. Communication between partners is required for consent to be part of sexual intimacy. If two people are too nervous to communicate or if they feel that they can't communicate with each other, then they shouldn't have sex. If one person is unable to communicate (say, because of having passed out), then consent, by definition, can't be expressed. Sex is a communicative act, in other words. This is what we are implicitly teaching our students and our community when we advocate for consent.

Sex Is Nonviolent. Violence can take many forms. It can be physical or emotional. Violence disregards another person's agency, silences another person, enacts harm on another person (physical and/or emotional). To reduce another human being to the level of an object, or to use a person without regard for her or his wishes or desires is a form of violence. This is what we are implicitly teaching our students and our community when we advocate for consent.

Sex Is Respectful. To expect consent to be given in situations of sexual intimacy is to acknowledge that each person is deserving of respect. That a baseline level of respect between partners is necessary. That respect for human dignity is required. That because sex makes everyone vulnerable, it requires heightened concern for one's partner. Respect is implied within consent because consent is an act of respecting another person's wishes, desires, agency, and physical and emotional well-being. This is what we are implicitly teaching our students and our community when we advocate for consent.

Sex Is a Complex Aspect of Our Humanity. To understand consent also requires respect for the complexities of sex as a part of our humanity. To understand the sexual agency and desires of another person implies that both partners have given thought to who they are as sexual beings. Part of acknowledging this complexity involves attending to and doing our best to understand different stages of sexual development, uncertainty, and maturity. This is what we are implicitly teaching our students and our community when we advocate for consent.

Consent Is Empathetic and Compassionate. If it weren't, no one would have to worry about the ways that sex can hurt us. Consensual sexual intimacy is intimacy that respects the role of emotions during and following sexual activity, and understands that checking in with one's partner's well-being, both physical and emotional, is an act of compassion.[2] Nonconsensual sex carries with it long-term emotional implications, which is one of the reasons consent is so important. This is what we are implicitly teaching our students and our community when we advocate for consent.

Consent and Social Justice Are Connected. When we talk about consent, we are implying that everyone has rights within situations of sexual intimacy. People have the right to have their voices heard and respected. They have the right to have their bodies respected, and for their bodies to be treated as worthy of human dignity. They have the right to participate and also the right to stop participating, or to not participate at all. They have the right not to be objectified. Consensual sexual intimacy does not reduce the body and the person to inanimate objects. Consensual sex does not cause one's partner suffering and trauma. Consensual sex promotes human flourishing, hears a partner's voice, respects his or her wishes, and acknowledges her or his personhood. A culture of consent does not shame and blame a victim for having spoken up about an assault or trauma. This is what we are implicitly teaching our students and our community when we advocate for consent.

Consent Respects and Is Inclusive of Sexual Diversity. Sexual diversity can mean many things—a variety and range of sexual orientations and genders, but also a variety of paths for sexual activity and paths toward relationship. Sexual diversity is inclusive of sexual abstinence. A culture of consent does not advocate a one-size-fits-all sexuality. Consent is inclusive of many types of and approaches to sex, including deciding not to have sex. This is what we are implicitly teaching our students and our community about sex when we advocate for consent.

Consensual Sex Is Ethical Sex. There is no such thing as having sex without ethical implications. To have sex with another person is to step into the realm of ethics, because anything that involves another person has ethical implications. This is what we are implicitly teaching our students and our community when we advocate for consent.

Consent in Practice Is Always in Flux. It can be given one moment and taken away the next. It can involve words or gestures. Because it is in flux, to attend to consent requires continual attention toward one's partner. This is what we are implicitly teaching our students and our community when we advocate for consent.

Educating about Consent Makes Sex into a Community Issue. When we educate about consent, when we require consent, when we speak of the implications if consent is not given, we are deciding to place sexual ethics at the center of our community life. We are legislating ethics. We are asking everyone in our community to be attentive, aware, and respectful of this issue. This is what we are implicitly teaching our students and our community when we advocate for consent.

Consent implies a lot, in other words, surely even more than I've included here. It expects a lot from community members—a lot of commitment, understanding, respect for one's partner, a serious reflection on the meaning of sex. When communities prioritize consent, they are acknowledging that sex always has meaning. If sex were truly meaningless, then consent wouldn't matter because hurt and pain and violence and trauma would never be at issue. When you look at all that consent implies and all that it expects of us, you can begin to see what a paradox it sets up for hookup culture. You can't get around hookup culture when you're educating about consent—you have to upend its norms, scripts, and values. When you look at all that consent implies, you realize how problematic our cultural scripts are around masculinity, around the double standards, name-calling, and victim blaming so many women face on campus. When you look at all that consent implies, you start to realize how much we need to rethink sex education overall, and not just on campus. We need to rethink it as people who are united in our concerns for the basic well-being of our children and students, for their healthy sexual development—united in our efforts to combat sexual violence.

Fifth: Not Allowing Consent to Trample Rights and Religious Commitments

One worry I've encountered among students I've spoken to over the years has to do with the presumption of sex in our campus programming about it—that everyone is having it and will have it during college. These students worry that this exacerbates the pressure to have sex and problematic assumptions about sex. It seems to see sex as a given for *all* students. For many students, it likely is a given. But not for all. Devout Muslims, Orthodox Jews, Mormons, and many committed evangelical Christians and conservative Catholics do not plan to and will not have sex during college, and they often feel that they are disrespected because of this by their peers and even by their institutions. Their universities, they feel, have chosen priorities around sex that exclude them, or sometimes even mock them. There are also students who simply don't feel ready or do not want to have sex during college—a decision that has nothing to do with religion at all. The presumption that all college students have sex, reinforced by the way in which we educate around sex and consent, perpetuates this narrative.

The presumptions we make in our sex education on campus exacerbate the notion that everyone is always having sex at college. Perpetuating this norm only puts more pressure on students who already feel so much pressure around sex.

So, I will make one more addition to the preceding list.

Prioritizing Consent Does Not Presume Everyone Is Having Sex. For a community to privilege consent is for it to acknowledge the pervasiveness of sexual violence and the need to prioritize values that work against the perpetuation of violence. Prioritizing consent does not assume that all college students are or should be engaging in sexual intimacy.

I wish I could add, as I did with all the others, that "this is what we are implicitly teaching our students and our community about sex when we advocate for consent." But I don't think that's true at the moment. If it were, I wouldn't hear so many complaints from students about it.

Acknowledging a Framework for Sexual Ethics Is Only a Start

This is, I hope, a good start, but it doesn't yet get at systemic sexual violence or address the problematic, inherited scripts and narratives embedded within our communities. This is the task that is up next.

8 | SCRIPTING CONSENT
AN ACTIVIST LESSON PLAN

When Interrupting Is a Good Thing:
Applied Hermeneutics and Feminism

The topic of my PhD dissertation might be considered obscure given the kind of work I do now. It's based on the work of postmodern feminist philosophers of religion, including Grace Jantzen, Luce Irigaray, Hélène Cixous, and Julia Kristeva. Reading these thinkers is not for everyone, but I loved them, still love them, will always love them. Even if they might sound far from relevant to the research I've done in the last decade, their influence is everywhere in my work.

And here they are again. Why?

One of the things that fascinated me about these philosophers was their writing—literally the way it was structured on the page. A central idea in their work is the notion of rupture and interruption—that we must interrupt the oppressive structures of culture and society, and we must interrupt and rupture (break through) the narratives, scripts, and stories that serve to oppress. Interrupting these narratives is paramount if we are going to identify the oppressive and patriarchal forces operating in our stories in order to transform them and society and culture along with them—especially the violence structured with these forces. For Grace Jantzen, this interrupting is central to the goal of human flourishing—central to the work of social justice, to put it more plainly. Kristeva went so far as to interrupt texts with her own voice and writing in the margins, creating new columns and spaces for her critique of the preexisting text.[1]

All this is to say: one of the most important and practical things I learned from these feminists was the importance of interrogating a story and language and revealing their effects on culture and society. This is necessary work—paying attention to scripts, to narratives, to the way we talk (literally the words we use) about what we believe we should be doing—if we are going to transform our communities toward the end of justice, empowerment, and liberation. If we are going to tackle violence toward the end of eliminating it. This method can be applied to the cultural narratives and scripts that perpetuate and enable sexual violence.

Interrogation and interruption are good, indeed necessary. Interruption is essential if we want to transform our communities toward a specific end. And I hope it's clear by now that the scripts and narratives that young adults and college students inherit about sex (with all those "shoulds" and "musts" and "not allowed tos") need a lot of interrogation and a good deal of interruption so that the culture of sexual violence can be revealed and a culture of consent can supplant it.

This work is social justice work. It is activist work. It is work toward the development of a clear attitude and framework for sexual ethics. It is the work we need to do, and it must be done both by individuals and by communities. It cannot be done, and we should not allow it to be done, by university lawyers.

At the heart of the university is a commitment to the common good. But how can we truly commit to the common good if we've never sat down to ask ourselves how that commitment reveals itself and functions among us—or is ignored, is trampled, or is absent in certain corners of university life? And isn't it also true that at the heart of the university—of its role and purpose in our society—is a commitment toward the common good beyond its own walls? Don't universities have a responsibility to engage issues that affect the common good more broadly—issues like sexual violence?

Step 1: Advice on Creating a Safe Space for Discussion

So, how can we do a better job of educating about consent?

With any sensitive, personal subject, getting a group of people to feel comfortable talking to each other when they've just met or don't know each other well is not an easy feat. It takes time for the group members to develop a rapport, to begin to trust one another, to be willing to open up and be honest, or, at least, more honest than they would be initially. This takes investment on the students' part and on the group leader's part, which also means on the institution's part. The kind of "lesson plan" I offer here is not something that can be done by herding hundreds or thousands of people into a room for a one-time, hour-long sex talk.

What I am suggesting that we do goes far beyond what passes for consent education on today's campuses. But it could help us to confront and transform systemic violence in our communities, so why wouldn't we try it? The structure for doing exactly what

I suggest already exists: the classroom and the syllabus. It's just a matter of each community deciding to open up these existing structures for this purpose.

In my own classroom, when I teach on issues related to sex, hooking up, and other topics that are deeply personal, I hope that my students can trust each other enough by the end of the semester to be at least somewhat honest. In a few lucky instances, I've had students who've truly bonded with one another and have had what I would regard as transformative, life-changing conversations during the semester we've spent together. This is the ideal. But we have to be willing to do our best and hope for the best with each new group of students.

I never expect students to share personal stories with me. I don't ask for them, ever, though students are always allowed to offer them if they feel comfortable. I don't want students to be put in a position where they feel pressured to talk about personal topics or to confess their secrets. (Though there are certainly institutions I've visited that try to set up situations in which students meet me—a stranger—in a private room to "chat openly," the idea being that I am going to somehow gather up all the information on what is really going on and pass it along so the university knows what's what, which I always decline to do.)

So, if we are going to talk about deeply personal subjects, without asking anyone to first contribute deeply personal stories, how do we actually begin this conversation?

We can employ the stories of others from literature, ethnography, memoir, and qualitative sociological and psychological research. Plenty of stories already exist on the subjects we need to discuss. These stories can be the springboards that allow us a way in to a difficult conversation, offering us a means for talking about a subject without revealing ourselves directly in the process.

Take Amy, the student to whom I refer in the introduction. I tell a much longer version of her story at the beginning of my book *Sex and the Soul*. Many students, faculty, and staff have brought up Amy over the years: her story, what she says, who she is, what she's like, how they know people who are just like her or who have had experiences similar to hers. Reading Amy's story empowers people to talk about some of the most difficult issues any of us might face during college. It gives them something to hold on to as they navigate a conversation not only about hooking up but also about consent and sexual assault. When people talk about Amy, they may indeed be talking about something very personal, but they are able to talk about these subjects, to analyze them, without also saying, "This is something that happened to me, too."

When I begin a semester with a classroom full of new students, my goal is to find as many relevant stories as possible that will become springboards for our discussions. I draw them from all over—from memoirs, novels, academic ethnographic and sociological research, serious nonfiction, as well as my own research and interviews. I pull stories from philosophy and religion and psychology, from something I've heard on National Public Radio, or from a documentary or movie I've seen. I do my best to present a diversity of stories about people who represent a diversity of genders, sexual orientations, racial and ethnic backgrounds, and religions. I try to use sources that my students can grab onto so we can have a conversation about the issues at hand, without forcing students to discuss things they might not want to. That said, if students want to talk about personal topics, they are welcome to do so, as long as they can do it in the context of the discussion about the relevant readings and resources we are using at the moment.

To me, this is one basic method for creating a safe space. It takes a willingness to sustain a discussion over time with students. It takes some good resources to spark discussion and reflection. It takes planning and thought to find a diversity of resources to open the conversation and to establish the notion that it is OK to consider the personal in relation to the texts under discussion.

One last thing on safe spaces: there is a lot of talk on college campuses about trigger warnings and the fear that we're coddling our students, that our students are asking to be sheltered from certain topics. I have never used trigger warnings myself. I'm of the mindset that, in an ideal world, even if something is incredibly personal and therefore difficult, it is better to talk about it than not, or at least, it is better to be in the presence of texts and people who talk about it than not. This is the only way for us to integrate, contemplate, and move through those difficulties—to disarm them as best we can. The process will likely be painful and involve some, or maybe much, discomfort. But there is liberation and empowerment to be had in going through this process. My "warning" to students about the course topics at hand is the list of readings and topics outlined for each class session on the syllabus, along with a short discussion at the end of each class about what comes next—but I don't think of my syllabus and these notes about upcoming readings as "trigger warnings."[2]

That said, I'm not against trigger warnings, and I am very sympathetic to the difficulties posed by trauma. I would never force students into situations they are not ready for or cannot tolerate. If a student came to me and said she or he couldn't participate in a certain discussion of a reading or topic but wanted to talk to me about why, I would listen and do my best to understand. But I still believe that the best way through—the most transformative way through—is to be in and among, to be in the presence and in the face of, those things that challenge us and that reach the deepest, most painful parts of who we are.

Step 2: Putting Our Own Diverse Stories on Paper—Creating a Canon

The next thing we need to do in each of our communities—and every college community is different—is to invite members of the community to write down the inherited stories about sex, relationships, hooking up, and so forth that are operating on campus. We can begin this process in private—alone, in a journal, on one's phone or laptop—but ultimately the goal is to get a sense of the wider stories that influence student realities and experiences. Only then can we begin to take stock of these operating narratives, to open them up to critique and discussion and to understand the biases around gender, sexual orientation, race, and so forth that run through them.

Here, I am speaking about those stories students learn that are full of "shoulds" and "musts" and "supposed tos." These may be stories that students learn prior to college, such as cultural and societal expectations about what college is "supposed to be," but I also mean the stories they inherit upon arriving on *this* specific campus. These are the most important stories of all because they are the ones that students employ in their real lives. Thinking of them as scripts is helpful, especially if they are taken literally: How do we perform (because they are performed) the expectations, ethics (or non-ethics), desires, and so forth that are handed down to us in our social and sexual lives?

Of course, the question is: How do we ask for these narratives from students, safely? I just spilled a lot of ink on not requiring confessions.

There are ways to get at the operating narratives and stories of a community without asking for a personal, specific story from each student. The objective should be to get at the narratives that students inherit on a collective scale, such as the story the students at the Midwestern college told me about how hookups were "a competition to see who can care the least," or the story the students from the sexual working group at the liberal arts college told about what they were "allowed" and "not allowed" to do now that they were in college, and how the sign that a hookup was "over" and that people could finally go to bed was when "the guy comes." These were not the specific stories of individuals but instead were the scripts and stories to which students felt everyone was expected to conform.

We can get at these stories by asking questions about how people get together, how hookups happen, the role of drinking, or a typical night at a party. What priorities, expectations, and gender roles are involved? When I was in college, we used to joke about Joe and Jane Hoya—supposedly the quintessential male and female Georgetown students. So, to use this as an example, you could say to students at Georgetown: So, Joe Hoya is a first-year student. Tell the story of his ideal night at a party, and how he goes about finding someone to hook up with. What is his attitude toward his partner? How does it all happen, beginning to end? Is he sober or drunk? Is he sober but pretending to be drunk? What is the role of alcohol overall? And so forth.

Asking students to consider particularities in these stories is essential. What about if Joe Hoya is black? White? Latino? Gay? What if Jane Hoya is lesbian? Transgender? Bi? How are scripts different for women? Men? First-years? Seniors? How does economic background affect things? What if a person is in a fraternity or a sorority? What if someone is not? What is the story for athletes, and does that story depend on the particular sport and team of which an athlete is a part? What if a student is Muslim? Jewish? Christian? Catholic? Do any of these particularities influence the way the story is handed down to certain groups, and if so, how? And does the script/inherited narrative depend on the group? Are some groups not affected or even considered in the handing down of scripts? Are some groups rendered invisible by these narratives? Why might this be?

Essential topics to address in this process of collecting narratives include the specific campus scripts around the following:

1. Drinking (in general)
2. Pregaming (getting ready for the party)
3. Partying (including specific fraternities and sororities if Greek life is part of campus)
4. Hooking up
5. Tailgating
6. Pledging (on Greek campuses)
7. Gossip (following all of the preceding topics)

The ultimate goal of this endeavor is to have members of the community—small groups of students under the guidance of a faculty member, administrator, or staff member—gather the narratives and scripts that most influence sexual decision-making and activity on campus. The community should be as thorough as possible in collecting a diversity of stories and should utilize additional stories that address certain constituencies if relevant (e.g., athletes are exempt from x, y, and z for this reason, or Muslim students receive this story instead).

I want to emphasize that doing this work does not have to be a horrible chore full of doom and gloom. It can be difficult and painful, but it also can be fun and playful. Many of the conversations I've recounted here were told with lots of laughter, eye-rolling, and joking—and not because the students were being disrespectful. By articulating these scripts out loud, the students were able to laugh at some of the ones they thought were ridiculous (even if they followed them) or admit that what they practiced involved a paradox of beliefs and conflicting desires. Sometimes it's a relief to get things out on the table, since they may look less sinister when they are sitting there in front of everyone in the bright light of the day. It's a way of disarming what can be incredibly difficult material because everyone is in it together, and there can be relief in acknowledging this.

The overall goal is to create a canon of scripts and narratives for that specific campus—one that students will then analyze, critique, and ideally, interrupt in order to challenge systemic norms that promote sexual violence and harassment. The act of articulating these narratives—of students actually writing them down in a form that can be read through like a story, and doing so in ways that are serious, or sometimes even playful, but most of all that can be contemplated, discussed, unpacked, and analyzed—is intended to be empowering. It gives students the opportunity not only to identify these narratives and scripts but also to take control of what was previously beyond their control. To make explicit what previously may have been implicit, by writing it down and having it there to see, to read, to take home and think about. To talk about with friends. To manipulate and change. To set aside as undesirable. To transform into something new and different, better and more respectful, more life-giving, more fulfilling.

Step 3: Coming to Terms with Consent on (Each and Every) Campus

This next part of the process is where the work of research, reading, and critical, intellectual reflection is paramount. To interrupt, rupture, or break through the operating scripts and narratives on campus requires figuring out what to use to do the interrupting. *Which* values, *which* ideas, *which* approaches to ethical relationship will provide the framework to critically evaluate and unpack the biases and expectations embedded in these narratives? Which tools and criteria will help to best reveal how stereotypical ideas about gender, sexual orientation, race, and so forth are operating in these scripts? In the previous chapter, I provided a list of operating values embedded in the implied sexual ethics of consent as I see it. But you can have the students brainstorm this list as well, on their own, and with the help of additional texts.

To assist in this part of the process, I suggest turning to four types of resources—and using them all:

1. **The University Mission and Vision Statement**—because this (supposedly) provides the community with a shared vision. It will introduce any relevant religious commitments into the conversation, if the school has a religious affiliation. It is a statement of community ideas and commitments, so why not start there and actually use it? Also, when people choose to attend or work at a college, they are by default agreeing to be in a community that holds this vision. People might as well take a look at what they've implicitly agreed to.

2. **The University Policy on Consent and Sexual Misconduct in the Handbook**—because everyone should read (really, carefully, read) this statement and discuss its requirements and expectations, since, whether they like it or not, whether the policy is well written or not, everyone on campus is subject to it.

3. **Readings in Literature, Philosophy, Ethics, Religion, Feminist Theory, Social Justice, Psychology, and So Forth**— because when we are thinking about who we would like to be, and what kind of community we would like to have, it's helpful to read what others from a diversity of backgrounds have said and thought. Not to be prescriptive, but to get a sense of what possibilities are out there, and which values and criteria we feel committed to and might draw on to evaluate our scripts.

4. **Soul-Searching on the Part of the Students**—because, in an ideal world, this is an opportunity for all of us to think about who we are, how we act, and whether those two things align. Having an opportunity to reflect on our hopes and aspirations, and how we act in relation to others around us—in light of all the resources mentioned earlier—is an experience that most college students are longing for but rarely get. This is a chance

for each participating member of the discussion to think deeply about the buildings blocks of ethics.

The goal of this process is to develop a set of values or criteria for a framework for sexual ethics that privileges consent—one specific to the needs and particularities of this campus.

If the preceding seems like it will take a lot of time and effort, as well as resources—especially intellectual resources—that's because it will. But if we care about these issues, and if we care about sexual liberation (whatever that might mean, depending on one's background and one's ethical and religious commitments), and if we care about educating our students about consent, then we should take the time to investigate these kinds of resources and set them against the operating, inherited experiences and scripts on campus. The good news for those of us who work at a university is that doing this work is supposed to be what a university is for.

Going through this process is a form of community activism. Community activism not only is something we export across the street and to far-flung locales but also should involve taking the values and reasons that make us want to be activists and applying them to our own communities, ourselves, and our peers by asking: Do we adhere to these values and commitments at our parties, in our hookups, with our friends and peers on the weekends? And if not, why not?

Another Interlude: On Appealing to University Mission Statements

I want to devote some space to those mission and vision statements that all universities boast of on their websites and explain why we should pay attention to them when we are having this conversation. Just like the codes for sexual misconduct and consent from the student handbook that often go unread and unprocessed by the majority of the community, so too these proud university mission statements are often ignored. Why? Why do we have them if we don't bother to use them or even look to see what they say (even if it's to critique them or disagree)? Why do we ignore them when they are so full of idealism and the positive expectations that our communities have for us? These statements often speak of leadership, transformation, service, and this notion of the "common good," which are helpful concepts to consider when thinking about who we want to be as human beings, and as sexual beings, within our communities. And by the way, most athletic departments—including athletic powerhouses like Big Ten and ACC schools—also have mission and vision statements of their own. They are there to complement and further the umbrella university mission statement. Shouldn't all of us be reading about these expectations, ideals, and hopes for our athletes—even if we aren't athletes ourselves?

At the moment, we seem to avoid appealing to university mission statements in the same way we avoid delving into the subject of sexual ethics. Making claims about ethics makes us nervous because we are afraid of imposing or offending. But mission and vision statements are statements of ethics. In order to discuss consent, we need a structure (at least *some* structure) for ethical sexual decision-making, and we already have operating statements about ethics that supposedly ground our campuses. Let's put them to work toward helping us reflect on sexual decision-making and consent, even if we come to find that we disagree with them.

Let's look at mission statements from five schools: Harvard (an elite, private college), Georgetown (because it's my alma mater and also a religiously affiliated institution), the University of Texas (because it represents a big public state system of fourteen institutions), Florida (because it's a big sports school and has been mired in controversies over its mishandling of sexual assault), and, finally, the Michigan State athletic department. All these institutions have lofty and aspirational statements—a good thing, when we are trying to challenge problematic cultural norms that perpetuate sexual violence.

Harvard's mission statement speaks of educating "citizens and citizen-leaders" and describes how its classrooms are places where students can "embark on a journey of intellectual transformation." It prizes diversity and tolerance, and emphasizes how, through diversity, "intellectual transformation is deepened and conditions for social transformation are created." It concludes by stating several goals: that students will become self-aware and find purpose for "their gifts and talents," that they will assess "their values and interests," and that they will learn "how they can best serve the world."

The University of Texas's mission statement—in addition to its mandate "to improve the human condition in Texas, our nation and our world," to respect diversity, to "shape public policy for the common good," and to turn out graduates "with a sense of service and the ability to lead"—includes a declaration of community "ethos." Among other things, this ethos statement speaks of building "trust through our actions," both "personal and professional." It also sets high standards for the community: "Our actions are moral, legal and ethical and we hold ourselves accountable when we fail to achieve this standard."

Florida State, in addition to its general mission statement, has what's called "The Seminole Creed," which is a statement of "values and morals at Florida State University" and includes a "guiding ethical norm," which is "responsible freedom." This statement reads like a pact among community members that begins with, "As a member of this community, I promise the following." Next comes a list of core values, which includes truthfulness, respect, excellence, freedom of speech and inquiry, diversity, justice, citizenship, and discovery. Under "justice" is the corresponding promise: "I will treat others in a fair manner and strive to make the university a community of justice." Under citizenship it states: "I will act as a responsible citizen in the university and beyond, participating in those activities fostering citizenship."

Georgetown's mission statement immediately mentions that the university is Catholic and Jesuit—but also "student-centered" and research-oriented. It argues that "serious and sustained discourse among people of different faiths, cultures, and beliefs promotes intellectual, ethical and spiritual understanding." The university prizes diversity and a "commitment to justice and the common good" and hopes to graduate "reflective lifelong learners" who are "responsible and active participants in civic life" and who "live generously in service to others."

Finally, Michigan State's mission statement for its athletic department declares that through athletics, "we gather and engage our community to teach, support and celebrate our student-athletes in their quest for excellence." The statement goes on to list "core values" such as respect, accountability, and integrity.

The reason I am presenting these statements and highlighting specific aspects of a university's mission and vision should be obvious by now. Each one of these statements grounds the university in commitment and service to the world, to justice, to values like respect, to fairness, to responsible citizenship, even to friendship. They are statements of ethics, of ideals, of hopes for the university as a whole and for each individual community member within it. They are rich with possibilities for reflecting on sexual violence, for the scripts and narratives that perpetuate it, and for transforming our communities into cultures that privilege consent. These mission statements can be used to reflect on a community's hopes, for what they would like to be, as well as to evaluate what's gone wrong when a university's actions reveal a failure to adhere to its own mission. These statements are meant to be used and contemplated by community members; if we do not use them, they amount to mere lip service—a lofty statement that ultimately means nothing. But I don't believe these statements exist just for show, so I believe we should use them accordingly.

Step 4: Interrupting Inherited Scripts and Rewriting the Stories We Pass On about Consent and Sex

After going through all this preliminary analysis—the reading of others' stories; creating a canon of stories specific to one's community; and exploring the criteria, values, and an ethical framework to ground a culture of consent—it's time to do some interrupting. In many ways the task is simple: take the list of criteria and values that the group developed as a framework for sexual ethics and consent on campus, and use it to evaluate the inherited scripts that the students have identified. The idea is to use the framework to critique those scripts, to interrupt their operating norms, assumptions, and expectations. To interrogate all those "musts" and "shoulds" and "not allowed tos." The ultimate goal is for the group to "rewrite" these inherited scripts and/or to create new scripts that reflect this framework for sexual ethics and consent—to create a new canon of operating stories.

My hope is that this process considers the diversity of students and unique student experiences while unearthing the biases operating within the campus culture and within our culture at large. The point is not to arrive at a one-size-fits-all approach to sexuality, or to ethics, but to open up the existing, inherited scripts to accommodate sexual diversity and diversity on many fronts, while at the same time empowering a community to come to terms with consent. This process invites students to do the difficult work of making choices about justice, about clarifying their expectations of each other and what it means to be a respectful, nonviolent community amid a diversity of attitudes and approaches to sex and relationships. It invites students to participate actively in the transformation of their communities, and to do so in the places where they live and socialize.

A Positive Cycle to Interrupt the Vicious One: Passing On Our New Scripts and Stories

I've written a lot about the vicious cycles in which universities and student populations find themselves. But although we can be caught in a vicious cycle of problematic, inherited scripts, we can interrupt it with new narratives and scripts. This process may indeed be a lot of work, but it is essential work.

The process I've described here is creative. Student groups are creative in the sense that they are being asked to write and collect the stories they've inherited and then rewrite them so as to produce new ones. But they are also creating a new set of scripts to pass on to their younger peers. With a group's permission, the canon of new stories can be used as primary texts for the next semester's students—those stories I mention in step 1 to be used in opening the conversation. These "inherited scripts" (or a selection of them) can then be evaluated, updated, revised, or set aside by the students in the new group when they discuss and write their own inherited scripts. Eventually, you have a student body engaged in contributing new scripts, aimed at privileging a culture of consent.

This process can also help to identify student leaders for the next wave of students who enter into this process—a diverse set of students will be able to work together with faculty, staff, and administration to facilitate the process for their newest peers.

This kind of engagement among members of our university communities will also help to remind everyone that the kind of critical, intellectual, and creative engagement that happens within our classrooms is not to be forgotten when people walk out the door but instead can be carried everywhere we go, such as to the parties we attend on the weekends, including while we are filling our red Solo cups from a keg or hooking up with someone we've just met.

I have visited many incredible university communities over the years—activist university communities, teeming with students who spend hours doing community service and who study social justice and related fields. Yet only rarely within these same communities do we take the tools and values that are so prominent within that work and apply it to our own actions, our own behavior, and the communities where we live and work. The method I suggest here for creating a culture of consent is one method for trying to get our communities to participate in the kind of reflection so many of them are already so good at, that so many of them already care so deeply about, but to put this to work toward the end of transforming our own communities around a specific issue like sexual violence.

Truly, the only thing stopping us is ourselves.

9 | THE ONLY THING STOPPING US IS US

CONTENDING WITH ONGOING
ACADEMIC BIASES AGAINST THE
PERSONAL

It Isn't Only Student Scripts That Require Interruption

Emma Sulkowicz's decision to carry her mattress around Columbia University for the entirety of her senior was incredibly moving and also intellectually astute. The mattress is a place where we are supposed to rest, to relax, to sleep, to burrow into on a cold winter's day for warmth and comfort. Our beds are where we go when we're exhausted, where we look for the reward and peace of sleep and dreams. The bed is also a place we go for pleasure with our partners, for physical and emotional intimacy, for connection and love.

That Emma Sulkowicz would take this object associated with peace and rest and pleasure, and face her community with the reality that, for her, her bed had become a source of trauma, of pain, of horror; that she would make her community contend with this for the entirety of an academic year, is profound. It was a performance that served as her senior thesis, which she called "Carry That Weight." The title has multiple meanings, referring to the mattress itself—cumbersome, big, awkward to lug around along with her books and other things, up and down stairs, squeezed into elevators. But the continual presence and bulk of the mattress metaphorically and literally sent the message that assault was a heavy burden. The mattress was a representation of the emotional, psychological weight Sulkowicz was carrying, and would have to carry forever. And one of her thesis's parameters invited other members of the community to choose to carry the mattress with her.

Sulkowicz's "performance" of her trauma via her senior thesis was brave—the norm is for women who are assaulted to retreat into silence, especially when they perceive that their university has failed them. Silence, shame, and isolation constitute the typical aftermath for women left to "carry the weight" alone. But what was especially brilliant about what Sulkowicz did was that she used the university's academic framework as the space for rupturing this typical narrative, which she rewrote into something completely new, claiming not only a voice but also a powerful platform for revealing the long-term impact of sexual violence. Sulkowicz used the intellectual tradition of academia to critique her own university's failure to adequately address sexual violence on her campus.

The administration at Columbia was not entirely appreciative that one of its undergraduates was using her talents to do exactly what undergraduates are supposed to do during their time of study.[1] I mentioned earlier the importance of "interruption," of rupturing the problematic narratives handed down within our communities that perpetuate and promote sexual violence. Emma Sulkowicz's decision to carry her mattress is a stunning example of this interruption—not only of student narratives but of the larger narrative and framework of the university and its administration. Her sheer presence wherever she went—the classroom, a party, the library, a cafe, the quad—interrupted the norms of regular university life, with a physical representation of sexual assault that everyone around her could see (even if they might try to ignore it). Sulkowicz sparked debate, conversation, approbation, and disapprobation alike. She opened a space in everyday life for sexual violence to emerge into the light, into the middle of everything. Once something is out in the open, it's difficult not to notice it and talk about it, and talk people did. Not just students, but faculty and staff and administration. And not just at Columbia, but across the entire nation.

On a much smaller and far more local scale, a group of my own students once engaged in this sort of academic interruption when they wrote and distributed a newspaper devoted to questioning attitudes and practices related to sex on their campus. The reason I mention them again is because in the mission statement for their newspaper, they called out the faculty, staff, and administration for not engaging them in rigorous academic discussions about sex and relationships—for leaving the students on their own to deal with this aspect of their lives. My students broke through the silence around sex at the university level in order to clear space for the open, honest, intellectual, and intergenerational discussion they desired. They called for the classroom to be opened up to this discussion and for faculty especially to join the conversations.

Sometimes it is our students who take on the work and responsibility for what our universities need to be doing to address sex on campus and all that goes with it. But we shouldn't be placing this responsibility on them or abandoning our students to guess and to flounder with these new policies we are writing and rewriting because of Title IX, in addition to the problematic scripts they inherit and are forced to grapple with. We need to open our doors to them—our classroom doors—if we truly hope to address sexual violence. To do that, many faculty members and administrators (maybe even most of us) must be willing to open our minds to what this requires of us as academic communities. It is a simple solution to use the classroom as a primary space for addressing sexual violence—after all, universities are centered around the classroom—but there is still a sense that the classroom is walled off from the rest of campus.

The Classroom: Still a Chilly Climate

Colleges and universities are first and foremost intellectual communities. They are where we go to become experts in a certain field, to understand complexity, to push the boundaries of knowledge toward new places and new heights. But they are also places where the personal, the subjective, and the experiential are still devalued, even after decades of feminists arguing that the personal is always political and vice versa; that the experiential, the social, and the relational are just as valuable and rigorous as the traditionally scientific and the so-called objective. The kind of project taken up by Emma Sulkowicz and what the students in my class are doing are of particular value, which is taking the personal and the experiential—the stuff of real lives—and viewing it through the lens of the critical, the intellectual, the academic, so as to better understand it, transform it, and lay it bare for critique and discussion. Projects like these should be regarded as academic and as evidence of universities operating at their best.

We must open up the intellectual domain to conversations about consent and sexual violence—and we must value those conversations at the same level that we value other subjects like mathematics and marketing. We must allow the "I," the "me," the "you," the "we," and the "us" into the work that our students do, in order to invite their real-life experiences into the domain of the critical and the thoughtful—and into the life of their minds.

It was in 1982 that Bernice Sandler and Roberta Hall published the now famous article called "The Classroom Climate: A Chilly One for Women?" about the subtly different ways women are treated—and devalued—in the classroom. "Men are more often viewed either consciously or unconsciously as the more valued students, the more important students," they write. "Thus teachers generally call on men more often, asking them more questions, and not calling on females as much, even when they raise their hands. White males generally get the most questions, then minority males, then white females, with black females receiving the least. Teachers generally pay more attention to male students. Faculty nod and gesture when males speak, but may look elsewhere when females talk."

Sandler and Hall go on to list some of the other issues: men get more offers of help, men are asked more open-ended, thought-provoking questions, and professors dislike the way women speak—often hesitant, overly polite. Women might cry if they get upset, and this is considered weak. Men are more likely to value competition, which wins them classroom success, whereas women are more likely to value intimacy and prioritize friendships, which don't. Professors are more likely to comment on a woman's "charm" or her outfit when calling on her. And then there is "the curriculum which often ignores women as authors or contributors or as subject matter." The authors also describe the devaluation of women faculty themselves. "Women faculty," they write near the end of the essay, "particularly if they engage in non-traditional teaching methods, may be evaluated more harshly by their fellow faculty members and by students."[2]

The college campus is still a chilly climate for many people. Though this has changed some and is still changing, the stuff that's stereotypically associated with women's experience—anything to do with relationships, intimacy, the personal—is still devalued in our classrooms. I have been amazed at my own students, how they are still being taught not to use the word "I" in their papers, as though they are not the authors of their work, and as though the personal, the subject, somehow diminishes and devalues their writing.

When I've brought up this issue with colleagues, they say that students don't know how to write critical papers from a personal perspective. While I understand this critique—since I spend a lot of my classroom time working with students on their writing—the answer is not to forbid the "I," to decenter it, to leave it outside the intellectual, because this perpetuates the disconnect between the intellectual and the practical. The answer, in my opinion, is to teach our students how to be subjects in those papers, how to bring themselves into the intellectual and critical work they do. This is not simply a symbolic gesture. When we forbid our students this basic thing, we reinforce the notion that the personal and the practical have nothing to do with the rational and the critical, that in fact they are disconnected; that the personal is ugly and messy and should not touch and soil the rational and the pristinely intellectual; that, in fact, students should check their lives and bodies at the door when they enter the classroom, and check their minds when they leave.

These priorities, these biases, have real implications for addressing sexual violence, consent, relationships, sex, and everything that comes along with them. Such subjects are some of the most personal and messy aspects of human experience, so it is easy to conclude that they do not belong in the pristine space of the college classroom, lest they dirty and defile it, lest they drag it down from its lofty levels. Academics will claim that the personal is too slippery to get a handle on, and so it does not make for a good or legitimate object of study. The list of reasons that we bar it from our intellectual spaces could go on and on, but the result of this devaluation is fatal for tackling systemic sexual violence and for the university project of educating our communities about consent.

Consent, sexual violence, sex in general—these are all complicated aspects of our humanity, of our being, of our society and our communities. If we want to transform our campuses into places where consent is valued, where sex is a respected and respectful act between partners, where sexual privilege is not something that one member of our community can wield like a weapon while others suffer, then we cannot shy away from how very complicated, rigorous, and intellectually demanding these subjects are. To understand these topics, we need to study them, using all the academic and intellectual resources at our fingertips and putting them to use toward this end. But we cannot do this work if we continue to dissociate the intellectual, rational, and critical from the personal, the social, the experiential.

Affirming the Connection between "Real Life" and the Life of the Mind

The other day, I found myself at a brunch with a friend and several people she wanted me to meet, one of whom is a professor at a prestigious university. My friend hoped that since we are both professors, we'd find we had a lot in common. What we found instead was that he and I are diametrically opposed in our understanding of a university education and the definition of what counts as intellectual, what counts as "real research," and who is a "real academic." He is a scholar of an eleventh-century thinker, and he spent the first part of our conversation bemoaning how unwilling his students are to show any interest in this person's writings. I asked this professor how he tried to connect this thinker to his students, his thought to their real lives, and to society today overall. This began a long, fairly uncomfortable (though quite lively) argument between the two of us about our very different pedagogies. He does not believe in relating any historical material to real life and considers the effort to do so a pathetic attempt on the part of a professor to pander to students (a failure, really, to be a respectable, legitimate professor). He considers such attempts outside the realm of "real" intellectual work. "Real" intellectual work and research are distinct from the practical, the everyday, and the messy lives of people. For him, the only "real" intellectual work is theoretical and esoteric, whether that theory is scientific or intellectual.

It became clear, over the course of our conversation, that he regarded my work—which deals in the very real, very practical stuff of students' lives—as lesser, and myself as not a "real" academic. These are deeply patriarchal attitudes about what counts as real research and what it means to be a true intellectual. This professor was establishing a hierarchy at the brunch table, with himself in the clear position of power, and me sitting squarely and firmly at the kids' table.

It is not as though I believe all faculty on campus must be engaged in practically applicable areas of inquiry that will have a direct influence on students' everyday lives. I have a deep respect and regard for all types of research, and as I noted earlier, my dissertation was about postmodern feminist philosophers of religion and their interest in medieval women mystics—not exactly the stuff of newspaper op-eds. But by establishing hierarchies and perpetuating patriarchal attitudes in academia, as though certain approaches and/or fields are more valuable than others, we are erecting barriers that prevent our universities from becoming the kinds of places our lofty mission statements describe. In the same way, these hierarchies and patriarchal attitudes are roadblocks to a culture of consent and the analysis necessary to build one up.

Real life is quite rigorous. Sexuality and all that goes with it are also quite rigorous. And consent—consent beyond "yes means yes" and "no means no"—is not something we can teach in an auditorium over the course of an hour with a few funny skits. But these biases that infect our university classrooms and our faculties like viruses contribute to the ongoing sickness of sexual violence on our campuses. These viruses affirm for our students that there truly is a divide between the life of the mind and the real lives that they lead outside the classroom—a divide between the rational and the emotional, between the intellectual and the personal. These biases affirm this divide and give it a stamp of approval. These biases teach students that it's acceptable to leave their brains at the door when they go to a party. They teach students to likewise divide themselves in two—as respectable, hard-working, thoughtful students during the day, and un-thinking, hard-partying, questionably behaving kids by night.

Two themes have emerged across all my research about college students. First, college students crave intellectually and critically rigorous resources, readings, and conversations about topics that directly relate to who they are and how they live. They'd like to talk about subjects like sex, including consent. They'd love classroom opportunities to do this, classes related to these subjects, and faculty with whom they could engage in these discussions and reflections. But, second, opportunities for inside-the-classroom reflection on these subjects are few and far between. At certain schools, students know of one faculty member (or two or three) who will engage these subjects and allow students to think critically about their own lives in this way. But these faculty members are rare. For the most part, students feel abandoned by the faculty and administration on their campuses to puzzle over these topics on their own.

As I always tell the Student Affairs staff on a campus where I am visiting: talking about sex with students is not for everyone, but it needs to be for some of us. At least some of us need to take up this work.

One of the simplest things faculty can do is to discuss the campus policy about consent and sexual misconduct within their classrooms. Not all faculty must do this, but some faculty must decide to. In effect, sexual misconduct policies are mission statements about sex and violence. They require unpacking and conversation. They deserve reflection and discussion, pondering, and, yes, questioning. These policies deserve a place in our classroom discussions in the same way as the honor code on cheating and plagiarism does. I don't mean simply tack the policy onto the end of our syllabi, as most of us do with the honor code and plagiarism policies—though adding it to a syllabus would certainly go a long way toward getting it in front of the eyes of all our students. I mean finding a spot during the semester, perhaps in relation to a reading or topic that we are teaching, where we can discuss the policy and its nuances in relation to our subjects. This will not work in every class, but again, at least some faculty need to be creative and intentional about finding and making space to discuss, question, and explore the meaning and nuances of these policies as topics for intellectual and critical reflection in and of themselves, how these policies reflect aspects of the course, as well as discuss the practical effects they might have on students' lives and decision-making.

For those of us who do take up this task in the classroom, on our syllabi, and with our students, it also must be made safe for faculty to do so. Just as students need safe spaces on campus for conversation and reflection, so faculty need a certain amount of safety to take up topics that are often, or at least currently, the third rail of academia—and by safe I mean legally, of course, but also professionally safe with regard to tenure.

Challenging Academic Biases against Certain Topics and Research

To encourage and empower faculty to make connections between the real lives of students and the topics they teach—whether this involves linking the experiential to class discussion, readings, and assignments, or if it involves becoming the central subject of the entire class—we need to fight biases against the practical, the personal, and the experiential as they relate to faculty getting tenure. Faculty in the humanities and in education have long had to fight for intellectual legitimacy. More difficult still is the situation for faculty who teach in areas that have to do with gender, relationships, and sex, and even more so if these topics (or any topic) have to do with children and young adults.

The academy tends to devalue and diminish research and teaching in these areas, making it doubly difficult for faculty members to convince a tenure committee that their work is legitimate and therefore tenure-worthy. These faculty must jump through extra hoops in the evaluation process in an effort to prove themselves. The result is that faculty, especially nontenured faculty, are discouraged from pursuing such topics and from teaching about them. (When I first decided to do my research about sex on campus, I was told by many colleagues that I was committing "academic suicide.")

The academy also buys into the notion that there is a hierarchy of audiences, which builds even more roadblocks to doing this kind of work. An academic audience is considered more valuable and therefore more legitimate than a nonacademic one. Ordinary people, people who do not have higher degrees or any degree at all, are considered the least valuable audience. This also means that if an academic decides to write to this audience (say, in a newspaper), their work will be dismissed as "unintellectual" and therefore devalued, and considered a "nonintellectual" activity. Even tenured faculty who write for a wider audience are often subsequently dismissed as "popularizers," as though their work has suddenly become tainted by the nonacademic "lower" class of readers they reach. The gendered, racial, educational, and economic biases in this hierarchy abound. But this "lower" and "less academically valuable" class of readers includes our students on the campuses where we work and teach. To prioritize one's students as a primary audience in one's work is to diminish one's chances at tenure, promotion, and respect among colleagues. To draw on students' experiences as one's subject for intellectual engagement is also a risk. The result is that student issues and realities are often sidestepped or overlooked as legitimate areas of inquiry. Identifying students as a primary audience is not simply discouraged; it can make a person's work not count as legitimate intellectual inquiry, or count less.

All these are ugly truths about academia, with implications for sexual violence on campus. If sex, if gender, if young adults, if our students are considered second-class citizens and second-class subjects in the pursuit of our intellectual and academic endeavors, how can we, as university communities, take on the challenge of changing the tenor of our campuses with regard to sexual assault and violence? The answer is that we can't. At least not enough of us can. It's too unsafe a topic. But the only thing stopping us—well, those of us who hold the power to change things—is ourselves.

Where Faculty Go Wrong with Student Affairs and Their Students, Too

There are also faculty biases about the realm of Student Affairs on campus—that messy space of residence halls and all that happens at night and outside the classroom. Academics and professionals whose field of inquiry is within the realm of student affairs and higher education have long bemoaned the perceived divide between the classroom and the residence halls, between the intellectual life on campus and everything else. The effort to bridge this divide has been a priority in student affairs departments at colleges and universities across the country for decades—the subject of conferences, journal articles, and books. Yet the divide persists, and it is due in no small part to the average faculty member's lack of understanding and respect for what professionals in Student Affairs do.

As a person working in Residence Life and living in the halls for six years while I was pursuing my PhD, I did not truly understand this divide until I became a tenure-track member of the faculty at a small, liberal arts institution. At my first campus-wide faculty meeting, I began to understand how deep the problem is, and how costly it is to our students. On the agenda at this meeting was the topic of spring break and the academic calendar. The faculty person leading the meeting explained that spring break had become linked to Saint Patrick's Day and would float according to where that holiday fell on the calendar. The reason for this change was that partying on Saint Patrick's Day had gotten so out of control and destructive that Student Affairs decided that the only real way to combat it was to get the students off campus for break.

As a former Residential Life person aware of how out of control students can become regardless of how amazing the professional and student staff are, I thought that this was a clever response to a terrible problem—which is that students on campus look for excuses (in this case Saint Patrick's Day) to binge-drink and become destructive.

What followed during this meeting was outrage on the part of the faculty. Student Affairs people had hijacked the academic calendar, and this was utterly unacceptable. The disparagement of Student Affairs staff was plentiful, with faculty arguing that Student Affairs staff clearly couldn't handle their jobs if their response to Saint Patrick's Day was to get students off campus. The faculty's sense of superiority was evident. Academics was their domain, and Student Affairs had to stay away. Not a single person wondered—if they were, indeed, going to "take back the calendar," which was their plan—how faculty might help Student Affairs staff cope on Saint Patrick's Day.

As I listened to this discussion, I thought: *this* is the divide Student Affairs people are always talking about. My fellow faculty members have no idea what it's like to live in the halls and deal with students at 3:00 a.m. when they are coming home from a party, nor do they care how difficult this is, or how they might help transform the situation for the better.

If we are to prevent sexual violence on campus, this kind of superior, dismissive attitude cannot continue. Faculty must stop pretending they have nothing to do with what happens when students leave their classrooms. Faculty must cease blaming Student Affairs for the persistence of sexual violence on campus, for the toxic presence of hookup culture, for an uptick in Title IX cases, for not "fixing" problems of sexual violence and education around consent—as though faculty have nothing to do with such problems. Many faculty turn a blind eye toward sexual violence in much the same way that university institutions have done until recently.

Sexual violence, assault, and harassment are systemic issues, and systemic issues require the attention and efforts of the entire community, especially those who are in power, and especially those who control all the intellectual spaces and domains where we might address such systemic problems. The most powerful people at university institutions are still the faculty (whether they feel this way or not). Faculty are in charge of critical thinking and reflection. Student Affairs can only do so much to end sexual violence without the help, respect, and efforts of the faculty. Disparagement is not helpful, and it displays an acute lack of awareness of the depth and complexity of the problem of sexual violence.

When I visit campuses, one of the things I always try to avoid is giving a lecture attended by students only. On many campuses, there exists the belief that we should corral our students into a room and give them a talking-to about sex, while the rest of us stand outside as though it has nothing to do with us. Every time the possibility of a students-only lecture comes up (which is quite often), I explain that this is the worst possible thing a community can do. To pile the students into an auditorium or a lecture hall and close the door behind them sends the following message that: Sex is your problem, and we're abandoning you to it. We don't care enough to sit with you while you think about it. You're on your own. I tell schools that one of the best and simplest things they can do to begin to transform and open up conversations about sex on campus and with their students is to show up. Attend the lecture about sex. Sit there in the audience, sprinkled among the students.

This one-hour effort is rewarded in spades. It communicates to the student community that sex is about all of us, not just them. We are all one community, and in this community we prioritize reflecting on and thinking critically about this part of everyone's life and this aspect of our campus. What is more, because I am here, sitting next to you, taking this in just as you are, I can be a conversation partner with you on this topic. We can continue the discussion afterward. Everyone in this room is a resource for you. We, the faculty and staff, care about this issue, too, and we are not abandoning you to it. It is as relevant to the intellectual life of this institution as any other issue. The best possible audience for a lecture about sex on campus, about sexual violence, about consent, about all that goes with it, is an audience full of administrators, staff, and plenty of faculty sitting among the students. Faculty are central partners in the effort to address and change sexual violence.

We need to build this bridge between faculty and Student Affairs, between real life and the life of the mind, and fast. If faculty do not participate in the solution, or refuse to, then they are part of the problem. Student Affairs can't do this alone, and faculty shouldn't expect them to. We are all one community, and we need to act as such.

CONCLUSION
CONSENT REQUIRES CLASS

What Does All of This Amount To?

Consent is an incredibly complex topic. But we need students to understand it in all its complexity: consent within a culture of hooking up; consent within the rape culture that dominates our communities; consent while we are drinking; consent while we are trying to have fun; consent while we are trying to do some sexual experimentation; consent as it relates to love, to pleasure, to sexual ethics. We must consider all of this if we want to do justice to consent (which we do, or say we do)—and to do this requires sustained attention and investment. How could it not? How could we possibly do justice to such a layered and myriad topic, how could we possibly believe we might tackle rape culture, that we might dismantle systemic sexual violence in our communities, with a single hour-long educational session for new students?

It's simple: We can't. It is impossible.

Yet we expect the impossible from the devoted Student Affairs professionals on campus who bravely and sincerely do the best they can with what few resources they've been given. At the moment, universities and colleges seem to believe that relying on lawyers and Title IX coordinators will dismantle rape culture and enshrine consent as a central value in their cultures. But university lawyers are there to protect the interests of the institution and to prevent public scandal. Title IX coordinators are there to help students, but also to make sure that reports get made and statistics are carefully updated and that the machinery of adjudication does its work so the university can prove to the government that all is well so that federal funding will continue to flow onto campus. Because attention to Title IX and hundreds of campus investigations have forced the issue, we have become very worried about process and legalities, but we've yet to devote enough effort to dealing with the education required to address consent in all its fullness and complexity within our student and community populations.

One of the most discouraging things happening because of Title IX and the scramble to check off that "consent education" box is the commodification of rape prevention. There is the outsourcing of sex education programming that has been going on forever, which is how events like "Sex Signals" and "Partying with Consent" have come to flourish. But there also is a growing body of products available to Title IX coordinators on campus—products to be bought and sold and tried out with students. There are "consent apps" to download and "box kits" that Title IX coordinators can purchase, with descriptions such as the following: "With more than 200-pages of content, the Investigation in a Box provides a tool like no other, placing training materials, sample templates and letters, reporting tools and case studies in your hands to assure you can meet the demands of a prompt, effective and equitable response to Title IX complaints and issues on your campus."[1] There are countless software programs and tutorials to educate students about sexual violence and harassment. There is big money to be made, in other words, in providing campuses with "for purchase" answers to sexual violence. But what these products are really for is proving compliance to the federal government: *sexual violence education—check*.

We Need to Do This the Old-Fashioned Way: In the Classroom

Luckily for those of us who work at colleges and universities, we already have all the tools we need to do the necessary education to tear down rape culture and replace it by building a culture of consent brick by brick. We don't need to buy any new products. Colleges and universities are replete with resources of every kind imaginable and some of the most brilliant minds around. We need to decide to focus those resources on dismantling the systemic sexual violence that infects our communities. Transforming rape culture into a culture of consent requires that we take on the analysis and critique of rape culture and the structures that enable it, that grip our campuses. It requires that we decide to do the work— the rigorous, intellectual work—of tearing it down and building something else in its place: a culture that privileges consent, sexual self-possession and awareness, and a respect for a diversity of human backgrounds, beliefs, and commitments.

We are not doing our jobs as academic communities if we are not addressing the needs and realities of the living, breathing, thinking, loving bodies that walk through our campus gates. It means we have failed to make our work relevant to the world and the people in it. It means we really are toiling away alone in the dark on subjects that no one cares much about and that mean little in the real world. It means we are so blinded by the obscurity of certain ideas that we've forgotten that ideas have meaning. Building a culture of consent is just as much an intellectual endeavor as it is a practical one. We need to stop making it a legal task, focused on the prevention of institutional scandal and the preservation of institutional funding. More regulation, more lawyers, more policies will not change a culture. Those things are there to hold people accountable, but they often do so in inhuman ways that lead to more injustices. The procedures we have now are notoriously problematic. Victims are often required to cede their rights, their freedoms, their voices, their power, their control, and their privacy in the hope of getting help and some measure of justice. Alleged perpetrators get little in the way of education, and due process is often ignored. Lawyers, Title IX, and adjudication should be a last resort. When we turn to adjudication, it is because our efforts at preventative education and dismantling rape culture have failed.

A culture of consent privileges education, which leads to cultural transformation—toward the just and the good and the humane. To tear down rape culture in order to build a culture of consent requires class. I mean this literally: cultural transformation needs to happen in the classroom. Colleges and universities are rich in classrooms and in professors to teach in them. We need to put these resources to use in creating a culture of consent. If we do not do this, it's because we have decided that addressing sexual violence in our communities is not a priority, that this subject isn't valuable enough to attend to. And this, in itself, is its own crime.

But it doesn't have to be this way. The answers lie within the purpose and idea of the university itself.

The Idea(l) of the University

The college campus is many things, but I'd like to think that it is still the place that so many of us go to discover and pursue our dreams, and to ask the Big Questions about life and meaning and purpose. Whether we are faculty or staff or administrators or students, the university pulls us in with its possibilities and opportunities and ideals. When I was in graduate school and also working in Residence Life, I read Sharon Parks's book *Big Questions, Worthy Dreams: Mentoring Young Adults in Their Search for Meaning, Purpose, and Faith*, and I thought to myself: Parks is right to push us—all of us who are tasked with teaching young adults, particularly in college—to remember that regardless of what our students are studying, they are still people who hope, who feel pain, who worry about the world and their place in it. For Parks, young adulthood, the period of life when many of us go to college, is a time when a new sort of meaning making begins. As she writes, "This mode of making meaning includes (1) becoming critically aware of one's own composing reality, (2) self-consciously participating in an ongoing dialogue toward truth, and (3) cultivating a capacity to respond—to act—in ways that are satisfying and just."[2] Young adulthood, according to Parks, ushers in a new kind of consciousness.

"How a young adult is met and invited to test and invest this new consciousness with its emerging new capacities will make a great difference in the adulthood that lies ahead," writes Parks. "The dreams that are made available, embraced, and nurtured, and the promises that are made, broken, and kept, will shape our common future."[3] Parks goes on to list a series of qualities pertaining to character and conscience that are at stake during the young adult years: "competence, courage, integrity, freedom, compassion, responsibility, wisdom, generosity, and fidelity," all of which are "qualities associated with exemplary citizenship, leadership, and the best of the intellectual life."[4] These are also the kinds of qualities that show up in the mission statements I discussed earlier. They are the kinds of qualities we need to instill in our conversations about consent.

Underlying consent, and a culture that privileges it, are some of the Biggest Questions of all, the greatest, most difficult inquiries that philosophers, theorists, writers, politicians, feminist thinkers, and scientists have made over the course of human history. The following list presents just some of the relevant Big Questions that we might consider in our efforts to address systemic sexual violence and build a culture of consent in its place:

What does it mean to be a sexual being?
How are we to understand gender identity?
How do sexual identity and gender coincide (or not)?
What is the nature of human desire? How does it work?
Can we control our desires?
Are there positive desires and negative ones?
What is the relationship (if any) between pleasure and sexual intimacy?

How have we constructed what it means to be a woman (femininity) and what it means to be a man (masculinity)?

How does growing up identifying as a woman affect sexual desire (if at all) and, with it, sexual decision-making?

How does growing up identifying as a man affect sexual desire (if at all) and, with it, sexual decision-making?

Why have we, as a society, come to associate women and femininity with sexual passivity and dominance?

Why have we, as a society, come to associate men and masculinity with sexual aggression and power?

What are the roots and causes of sexual violence?

What is the relationship between gender and sexual violence?

What are the structures that reinforce a culture of sexual violence in our world? In our communities?

What does it mean to be an "ethical" person? A "good" person?

What does it mean to be an "ethical" or "good" person who also has sex?

How does an "ethical" or "good" person act toward his or her partners?

What is the relationship between sexual ethics and consent?

What is the relationship between sex and human rights?

What is the relationship between sex and social justice?

What is the relationship between consent and human rights? Consent and social justice?

What are the stages of sexual development?

How do those stages correspond to sexual maturity and immaturity? To ambivalence and anxiety?

How do sexual maturity, ambivalence, and anxiety correspond to a person's ability to understand consent and give and gain consent during sexual intimacy?

What does it mean to love?

What is the nature of love?

What, if at all, is the relationship between love and sex?

What is intimacy?

What fosters intimacy? What destroys it?

What is the relationship (if any) between intimacy and sex?

What role do the emotions have in intimacy (if any)? In sex (if any)?

To what extent (if any) is a relationship necessary between two people for consent to be respected and understood during sexual intimacy?

What is consent?

What are the nuances of consent?

Can consent be given through gesture? If so, what gestures? Is it possible to determine which ones? Will the variety and creativity of expression always elude pinpointing these things?

Can consent be given through words? If so, what words? Is it possible to determine which ones? Will the variety and creativity of expression always elude determining such words and phrases?

This list of questions could go on and on. These are just some of the ones we might ask on campus—and by we, I mean all of us—faculty, staff, administration, those of us who have identified ourselves as the people who are going to take on and take up this conversation as part of our work. And by on campus, I mean everywhere across campus. These are the kinds of questions we need to be asking inside and outside the classroom, but especially inside along with our students. These are the kinds of questions that we should be using to frame our conversations about this topic from the moment our first-year students step onto campus for orientation, but also from the moment they enter their first university classroom to begin asking those Big Questions that college is about. We—faculty, staff, and administration—need to be empowering our students to make these inquiries, inviting them to consider these questions. They are rigorous, difficult, intellectual questions that get to the heart of the issues outlined throughout this book. They are also the very kinds of questions that are at the heart of the academic enterprise and our ideas about the university itself—if we allow them to be.

Universities are meant to be institutions that work for a better society and humanity, that work toward the "common good." Tearing down rape culture in order to build a culture of consent is one of those great common goods. The good, the just, the civil work of a university and everyone who studies and works within it should spill over into the wider world in order to change it and better it. That is why we have lofty mission statements that talk of turning out responsible and contributing citizens of the world. I believe not only that we can put a stop to sexual violence, not only that we can build a culture of consent, but that we must. Where else can we strive for these ideals, if not at our colleges and universities?

NOTES

INTRODUCTION

1. For Amy's story, see Donna Freitas, *Sex and the Soul, Updated Edition: Juggling Sexuality, Spirituality, Romance, and Religion on America's College Campuses* (New York: Oxford University Press, 2015), 3–9.

2. For an excellent introduction to the elements and analysis of rape culture, see, in its entirety, Kate Harding, *Asking for It: The Alarming Rise of Rape Culture—and What We Can Do about It* (New York: Da Capo, 2015).

3. The #MeToo hashtag has become synonymous with sexual assault and harassment in recent months, when a tidal wave of women began speaking out on Twitter (and other social media platforms) about their own experiences of sexual assault. Tarana Burke is the original author of the #METOO hashtag used by women to identify as victims and survivors. *Time* magazine reports that Burke is the "founder of a nonprofit that helps survivors of sexual violence, [and] created the #METOO movement in 2006 to encourage young women to show solidarity with one another. It went viral this year [2017] after actor Alyssa Milano used the hashtag #MeToo." Stephanie Zacharek, Haley Sweetland Edwards, and Eliana Docketerman, "TIME Person of the Year 2017: The Silence Breakers," *Time*, December 18, 2017, http://time.com/time-person-of-the-year-2017-silence-breakers/. See also Sophie Gilbert, "The Movement of #Metoo," *Atlantic*, October 16, 2017, https://www.theatlantic.com/entertainment/archive/2017/10/the-movement-of-metoo/542979/.

4. In December 2017, *Time* magazine named its Person of the Year "The Silence Breakers," who are the actresses who came forward to accuse Harvey Weinstein of sexual assault and harassment earlier in the fall of 2017.

5. See the Editorial Board of the *New York Times*, "What Congressmen Are Hiding," *New York Times*, November 17, 2017, https://www.nytimes.com/2017/11/27/opinion/congressmen-sexual-harassment-taxpayers.html.

6. See Elise Viebeck and David Weigel, "Rep. John Conyers Jr. Resigns over Sexual Harassment Allegations after a Half-Century in Congress," *Washington Post*, December 5, 2017, https://www.washingtonpost.com/powerpost/conyers-wont-seek-reelection-following-harassment-allegations-report-says/2017/12/05/17057ea0-d9bb-11e7-a841-2066faf731ef_story.html?utm_term=.0c84fba5ffbf.

7. For more on this, see Stephen Henrick, "A Hostile Environment for Student Defendants: Title IX and Sexual Assault on College Campuses," *Northern Kentucky Law Review* 40 (2013): 49–65.

8. See Brad Reagan, "Baylor Regents Found Alleged Sexual Assaults by Football Players 'Horrifying,'" *Wall Street Journal*, October 28, 2016, http://www.wsj.com/articles/baylor-details-horrifying-alleged-sexual-assaults-by-football-players-1477681988; see also Marc Tracy, "After Scandal, and with Staff Intact, Baylor Remains a Big 12 Power," *New York Times*, October 29, 2016, http://www.nytimes.com/2016/10/30/sports/ncaafootball/after-scandal-and-with-staff-intact-baylor-keeps-winning.html.

9. The *New York Times* published an excellent breakdown of the many ways Title IX is currently in flux according to the left-right political divide. For more on this, see the article in full: Anna Dubenko, "Right and Left React to Betsy Devos's Changes to Campus Sex Assault Rules," *New York Times*, September 12, 2017, https://www.nytimes.com/2017/09/12/us/politics/betsy-devos-title-ix.html.

10. Probably the most significant defense of hookup culture as key to women's future success comes by way of Hanna Rosin's book *The End of Men: And the Rise of Women*. In Rosin's article "Boys on the Side," adapted from her book, she likens young women becoming involved in a romantic relationship today to an unwanted pregnancy in the past, the argument being that relationships take time and investment away from a woman's focus on her career. "For college girls these days," Rosin writes, "an overly serious

suitor fills the same role an accidental pregnancy did in the 19th century: a danger to be avoided at all costs, lest it get in the way of a promising future." Rosin insists that women's liberation and pursuit of a career rest on the perpetuation of hookup culture. "To put it crudely," she writes, "feminist progress is largely dependent on hookup culture." Hookup culture allows women to have sex while eschewing emotional attachment, with the assumption that emotional attachment and vulnerability are obstacles to a woman's future success, an attitude that celebrates the narcissistic aspect of hookup culture—a position that I argue against in this book, precisely because of its implications for sexual assault. See Hanna Rosin, "Boys on the Side," *Atlantic*, September, 2012, https://www.theatlantic.com/magazine/archive/2012/09/boys-on-the-side/309062/. Kate Taylor, the author of "She Can Play That Game, Too," a widely circulated article about women at the University of Pennsylvania, makes a similar argument to Rosin's about hookup culture and its uses to women. See Kate Taylor, "Sex on Campus: She Can Play That Game, Too," *New York Times*, July 12, 2013, http://www.nytimes.com/2013/07/14/fashion/sex-on-campus-she-can-play-that-game-too.html?pagewanted=all.

Ariel Levy, however, the feminist author of *Female Chauvinist Pigs*, argues against exactly the sort of feminism and false notions of "sexual liberation" that Rosin praises—for Levy, this is feminism gone awry. Women don't want to be excluded anymore, argues Levy, but this has come to mean women turning themselves into the ready-made, patriarchal, sexual fantasies of men, without considering if this is truly what they themselves desire. "We are not even free in the sexual arena," writes Levy. "If we are really going to be sexually liberated, we need to make room for a range of options as wide as the variety of human desire. We need to allow ourselves the freedom to figure out what we internally want from sex instead of mimicking whatever popular culture holds up as sexy. . . . If we believed that we were sexy and funny and competent and smart, we would not need to be like strippers or like men or like anyone other than our own, specific selves." See Ariel Levy, *Female Chauvinist Pigs: Women and the Rise of Raunch Culture* (New York: Free Press, 2005), 200.

CHAPTER 1

1. For the April 2011 letter, see US Department of Education, Office of Civil Rights, "Archived: Dear Colleague Letter from Assistant Secretary for Civil Rights Russlynn Ali.—Pg 1," https://www2.ed.gov/about/offices/list/ocr/letters/colleague-201104.html.

2. For more on the Campus Save Act, see the website at http://campussaveact.org.

3. If and how more schools will come under investigation for Title IX violations under the Trump administration is still an open question, though the administration's Office of Civil Rights in the Department of Education said in its September 2017 "Q&A on Campus Sexual Misconduct," under "Question 12," that any resolutions and agreements schools made as a result of federal investigations are still binding, even if new interpretations of Title IX might call these investigations into question, and even if other schools are now not held accountable for what was previously considered a Title IX violation. The document states: "Schools enter into voluntary resolution agreements with OCR to address the deficiencies and violations identified during an OCR investigation based on Title IX and its implementing regulations. Existing resolution agreements remain binding upon the schools that voluntarily entered into them. Such agreements are fact-specific and do not bind other schools. If a school has questions about an existing resolution agreement, the school may contact the appropriate OCR regional office responsible for the monitoring of its agreement." It is unclear whether this mention of schools having "questions about an existing resolution agreement" leaves the door open for schools to simply ask questions or for reopening the agreement itself. For more information, see US Department of Education, Office of Civil Rights, "Q&A on Campus Sexual Misconduct," September 2017, 7, https://www2.ed.gov/about/offices/list/ocr/docs/qa-title-ix-201709.pdf.

4. See US Department of Education, Office of Civil Rights, "Questions and Answers on Title IX and Sexual Violence," April 29, 2014, https://www2.ed.gov/about/offices/list/ocr/docs/qa-201404-title-ix.pdf; US

Department of Education, Office of Civil Rights, "Q&A on Campus Sexual Misconduct," 7.

5. For the April 24, 2015 "Dear Colleague Letter on Title IX Coordinators," see US Department of Education, Office of Civil Rights, https://www2.ed.gov/about/offices/list/ocr/letters/colleague-201504-title-ix-coordinators.pdf; for the April 24, 2015 "Letter to Title IX Coordinators," see US Department of Education, Office of Civil Rights, https://www2.ed.gov/about/offices/list/ocr/docs/dcl-title-ix-coordinators-letter-201504.pdf.

6. For more information, see Association of American Universities, "AAU Climate Survey on Sexual Assault and Sexual Misconduct (2015)," September 3, 2015, https://www.aau.edu/key-issues/aau-climate-survey-sexual-assault-and-sexual-misconduct-2015.

7. For anyone interested in the subject of sexual assault on college campuses, especially in early research on the subject and how it's evolved, Mary Koss's work is essential reading. In particular, see Mary P. Koss, Christine A. Gidycz, and Nadine Wisniewski, "The Scope of Rape: Incidence and Prevalence of Sexual Aggression and Victimization in a National Sample of Higher Education Students," *Journal of Consulting and Clinical Psychology* 55 (1987): 162–70. Here, Koss and her coauthors not only deal with the fact of and the whys behind low rates of rapes reported to the police but specifically investigate the stunningly high percentage of women who report experiencing some form of sexual aggression and/or coercion during their time as college students—most of which do not get reported. "27.5% of college women reported experiencing [sexual assault] and 7.7% of college men reported perpetrating an act that met legal definitions of rape, which includes attempts," they write. "Because virtually none of these victims or perpetrators had been involved in the criminal justice system, their experiences would not be reflected in official crime statistics" (168). In this study, Koss and her colleagues looked at incidents of "sexual coercion" and "sexual contact," which is assault that does not include "penetration," but involves forced kissing, touching, and so forth. Koss is known for coining many terms related to sexual violence, including the notion of "hidden rape."

See also Mary P. Koss, and Cheryl J. Oros, "Sexual Experiences Survey: A Research Instrument Investigating Sexual Aggression and Victimization," *Journal of Consulting and Clinical Psychology* 50 (1982): 455–57; Mary P. Koss, "The Hidden Rape Victim: Personality, Attitudinal, and Situational Characteristics," *Psychology of Women Quarterly* 9 (1985): 193–212; Mary P. Koss, "Hidden Rape: Sexual Aggression and Victimization in a National Sample of Students in Higher Education," in A. W. Burgess, ed. *Rape and Sexual Assault II* (New York: Garland, 1998): 3–25; and Mary P. Koss and Mary R. Harvey, *The Rape Victim: Clinical and Community Interventions* (Thousand Oaks, CA: Sage, 1991).

8. The exact percentage of incidents of sexual assault among women on college campuses is the subject of tremendous debate and controversy, one that (generally) divides along political lines. Some conservatives think that this statistic of one in five college women, or even one in four college women, is incorrect because these numbers include assaults like forcible kissing (which certain parties consider as "lesser" assaults), attempted rape (or "incomplete" rape), and also is too general because the definition of what counts as sexual assault for many of these studies is broader than certain parties would like. The companion book for the film *The Hunting Ground* includes a thorough and excellent overview of this debate—but, of course, it comes down on the side of upholding those one in four or one in five statistics, as do I. There are too many solid academic surveys that uphold these statistics to engage in a debate that is, in my opinion, not a real debate. I refer anyone who is interested in pursuing this further to the overview of these statistics and the surrounding controversy to discussion of it in *The Hunting Ground*, which is comprehensive, succinct, and readily available online: Kirby Dick and Amy Ziering, "The Truth about Statistics of Sexual Assault in College," in *The Hunting Ground: The Inside Story of Sexual Assault on America's College Campuses*, January 31, 2017, http://thehuntinggroundfilm.com/2017/01/the-truth-about-statistics-of-sexual-assault-in-college/.

9. Centers for Disease Control and Prevention, "Sexual Violence: Facts at a Glance," 2012, https://www.cdc.gov/violenceprevention/pdf/sv-datasheet-a.pdf.

10. Bureau of Justice Statistics, "Campus Climate Survey Validation Study Final Technical Report," January 2016, https://www.bjs.gov/content/pub/pdf/ccsvsftr.pdf.

11. Amy Becker, "89 Percent of Colleges Reported Zero Incidents of Rape in 2015," May 10, 2017, https://www.aauw.org/article/clery-act-data-analysis-2017/.

12. RAINN, "The Criminal Justice System: Statistics," 2017, https://www.rainn.org/statistics/criminal-justice-system.

13. Association of American Universities, "AAU Climate Survey on Sexual Assault and Sexual Misconduct (2015)."

14. See One in Four USA, "Sexual Assault Statistics," 2017, http://www.oneinfourusa.org/statistics.php.

15. "Campus Sexual Assault under Investigation," *Chronicle of Higher Education*, 2017, https://projects.chronicle.com/titleix/investigations/.

16. For a detailed example of how mandatory reporting operates on a campus, see Purdue University's guidelines for its faculty, staff, and administration: "Mandatory Reporter Compliance Guide—Title IX—Purdue University," 2017, http://www.purdue.edu/titleix/compliance Guide/.

17. For more on the debate about mandatory reporting, see the following articles: Colleen Flaherty, "Faculty Members Object to New Policies Making All Professors Mandatory Reporters of Sexual Assault," *Inside Higher Ed*, February 4, 2015, https://www.insidehighered.com/news/2015/02/04/faculty-members-object-new-policies-making-all-professors-mandatory-reporters-sexual; and Tyler Kingkade, "Professors Are Being Forced to Reveal Sexual Assault Confidences, Like It or Not," *Huffington Post*, May 11, 2016, https://www.huffingtonpost.com/entry/mandatory-reporting-college-sexual-assault_us_57325797e4b016f37897792c.

18. Stanford student Brock Turner and the trial around his sexual assault of a female peer (known as Emily Doe) provoked outrage across the nation for the way concern for Turner on the part of the judge seemed to outweigh concern for the victim—even after the victim's 7,200-word statement about her assault and its effect on her life was presented to

the court. For coverage of these issues, see Liam Stack, "Light Sentence for Brock Turner in Stanford Rape Case Draws Outrage," *New York Times*, June 6, 2016, https://www.nytimes.com/2016/06/07/us/outrage-in-stanford-rape-case-over-dueling-statements-of-victim-and-attackers-father.html; Jasmine Aguilera, "House Members Unite to Read Stanford Rape Victim's Letter," *New York Times*, June 16, 2016, https://www.nytimes.com/2016/06/17/us/politics/congress-stanford-letter.html. For more coverage of Stanford's requirement that a panel be unanimous for a student to be held accountable for sexual assault, see Joe Drape and Marc Tracy, "A Majority Agreed She Was Raped by a Stanford Football Player. That Wasn't Enough," *New York Times*, December 19, 2016, https://www.nytimes.com/2016/12/29/sports/football/stanford-football-rape-accusation.html.

19. See US Department of Education, Office of Civil Rights, "Q&A on Campus Sexual Misconduct," 5.

20. I know this because I ask students during campus visits all the time, then I follow up by making sure that, yes, they did do all the required educational programming on their campus—it is often the consensus that, yes, we attended all the programming but, no, we've never seen the policy. "What does it say, anyway, and where can we find it?" they often wonder. Even those who've taken online tutorials about the policies will explain how you can just skip through them without really reading or paying attention and still pass the required quizzes at the end.

21. For the original article that resulted in the first Title IX complaint against Kipnis, see Laura Kipnis, "Sexual Paranoia Strikes Academe," *Chronicle of Higher Education*, February 27, 2015, https://www.chronicle.com/article/Sexual-Paranoia-Strikes/190351. For a succinct overview of Kipnis's two Title IX trials, see Jeannie Suk Gerson, "Laura Kipnis's Endless Trial by Title IX," *New Yorker*, September 20, 2017, https://www.newyorker.com/news/news-desk/laura-kipniss-endless-trial-by-title-ix. And for the full critique levied by Kipnis against Title IX, see her book *Unwanted Advances: Sexual Paranoia Comes to Campus* (New York: HarperCollins, 2017).

CHAPTER 2

1. This anecdote and its accompanying dialogue are told from memory. The conversation was not taped. I have done my best to remember it as it happened, both in content and in dialogue.

2. I write extensively about the effort to perform ambivalence in relation to sex, hookups, and partners, even though most students feel anything but ambivalent, in my book *The End of Sex: How Hookup Culture Is Leaving a Generation Unhappy, Sexually Unfulfilled, and Confused about Intimacy* (New York: Basic Books, 2013), 1–4, 55–74. Lisa Wade also writes extensively on this issue, in light of her own research about hooking up on campus, throughout her excellent book. See Lisa Wade, *American Hookup: The New Culture of Sex on Campus* (New York, Norton, 2017).

3. Jaclyn Friedman and Jessica Valenti are the coauthors of an entire volume devoted to precisely this issue, a book that is often taught and cited in this conversation about sex and consent on campus. See Jaclyn Friedman and Jessica Valenti, *Yes Means Yes: Visions of Female Sexual Power and a World without Rape* (Berkeley: Seal Press, 2008), in its entirety.

4. The job listing for the position of "interpersonal violence clinician and men's engagement manager," located in Princeton University's Health Services, read as follows: "The Interpersonal Violence Clinician and Men's Engagement Manager (Manager) will provide short-term clinical interventions and victim advocacy, and serve as the prevention specialist focused on mentoring and engaging men. The Manager will develop and implement men's programming initiatives geared toward enhancing awareness and challenging gender stereotypes, increasing the community's understanding of interpersonal violence dynamics, and reducing behaviors that lead to both perpetration and victimization. The Manager will also support the Director's prevention initiatives and assist in the provision of emergency response." For the full job posting, see "Interpersonal Violence Clinician and Men's Engagement Manager, University Health Services," *Inside Higher Ed*, May 29, 2017. https://careers.insidehighered.com/job/1387874/interpersonal-violence-clinician-and-men-s-engagement-manager-university-health-services/.

5. Recently, when I was teaching Shakespeare's *Measure for Measure* to my students at Hofstra University, I passed out copies of the school's consent policy as listed in the handbook and instructed the students to apply the policy to evaluate all parties involved in the play's "bed trick" scene (which involves swapping out one woman with another during a night of coercive sex, without the knowledge of the man, and making sure that sex takes place in the dark so he can't see his partner). The scene itself is a nightmare of nonconsensual activity and sexual coercion, but the students were both riveted by their school's policy (most of them had never even seen it before, much less actually read it) and also shocked to realize that a policy that came with such serious consequences if it was violated was so vague. They wanted *specifics*, such as how much alcohol *exactly* could they drink, and still give or gain consent? What body language *exactly* constituted a "yes"? When I told them that it depends on the situation, the person, and so forth, this stressed them out. I will return to this issue later when I discuss consent further.

6. I highly encourage a visit to Columbia's Sexual Respect website and resources: https://sexualrespect.columbia.edu.

7. During the time that Emma Sulkowicz carried her mattress across Columbia's campus, every major news media outlet in the country covered the story, with multiple articles appearing in the *New York Times*, the *Washington Post*, and the *Los Angeles Times* and coverage even on the *Today Show*. Googling Sulkowicz's name will elicit thousands of articles about her, about sexual assault on campus, and about Columbia University. A *New York Times* article from September 2014 provides a basic introduction to her reasons for carrying her mattress as well as some background on her claims against the alleged perpetrator and against Columbia's adjudication process. See Roberta Smith, "In a Mattress, a Lever for Art and Political Protest," *New York Times*, September 21, 2014, https://www.nytimes.com/2014/09/22/arts/design/in-a-mattress-a-fulcrum-of-art-and-political-protest.html.

8. Dr. Dorothy Edwards is the founder of the Green Dot Bystander Intervention Program. For more information about Edwards and about Green Dot, see her website: https://alteristic.org/services/green-dot/.

Green Dot and other bystander education programs have been particularly popular on Catholic campuses, precisely because of their social justice and community-centered ethic, and also because bystander education is basically the Good Samaritan in action. For an overview of Green Dot as a major campus initiative, see the description of it on the University of Notre Dame's website: https://titleix.nd.edu/green-dot/.

9. See Bethany Saltman, "We Started the Crusade for Affirmative Consent Way Back in the '90s," *The Cut*, October 22, 2014, https://www.thecut.com/2014/10/we-fought-for-affirmative-consent-in-the-90s.html. But as far back as 1999, scholars Susan E. Hickman and Charlene L. Muehlenhard credited Antioch College with sparking one of the first national conversations about consent. In their article from that year, they write of "traditional sexual scripts" that college students employ, which involve men initiating sex, and women playing the role of gatekeepers. In addition to offering definitions of consent, which include both verbal and physical forms, and the notion of "mental consent," which involves a "feeling of willingness" (259), Hickman and Muehlenhard point out that the complexity of consent goes far beyond "simply saying yes to a sexual initiation." "Most of the sexual consent signals in this study fell into identifiable categories of direct and indirect verbal and nonverbal consent signals," they write. "Participants who had previously engaged in sexual intercourse reported that they used a wide repertoire of signals to indicate their sexual consent in actual situations: direct verbal signals, direct nonverbal signals, indirect verbal signals, and indirect nonverbal signals. They reported almost never using statements about their level of intoxication or direct refusals to signal their sexual consent; they did, however, frequently convey consent by not resisting"(268). See Susan E. Hickman and Charlene L. Muehlenhard, "'By the Semi-mystical Appearance of a Condom': How Young Women and Men Communicate Sexual Consent in Heterosexual Situations," *Journal of Sex Research* 36 (1999): 258–72.

10. For more on this issue, and for more on consent in general, see the following articles: S. L. Dworkin and L. O'Sullivan, "Actual versus Desired Initiation

Patterns among a Sample of College Men: Tapping Disjunctures within Traditional Male Sexual Scripts," *Journal of Sex Research* 42 (2005): 150–58; C. L. Muehlenhard and Z. D. Peterson, "Wanting and Not Wanting Sex: The Missing Discourse of Ambivalence," *Feminism and Psychology* 15 (2005): 15–20; R. O'Byrne, M. Rapley, and S. Hansen, " 'You Couldn't Say "No," Could You?': Young Men's Understandings of Sexual Refusal," *Feminism and Psychology* 16 (2006): 133–54; R. O'Byrne, M. Rapley, and S. Hansen, "If a Girl Doesn't Say 'No' . . . : Young Men, Rape and Claims of 'Insufficient Knowledge,' " *Journal of Community and Applied Social Psychology* 18 (2008): 168–93; S. L. Osman, "Predicting Men's Rape Perceptions Based on the Belief That 'No' Really Means 'Yes,' " *Journal of Applied Social Psychology* 33 (2003): 683–92; T. Humphreys, "Perceptions of Sexual Consent: The Impact of Relationship History and Gender," *Journal of Sex Research* 44 (2007): 307–15; A. Moore and P. Reynolds, "Feminist Approaches to Sexual Consent: A Critical Assessment," in *Making Sense of Sexual Consent*, eds. M. Cowling and P. Reynolds (Aldershot, UK: Ashgate, 2004), 29–43.

11. Kristen N. Jozkowski, "Yes Means Yes? Sexual Consent Policy and College Students," *Change: The Magazine of Higher Learning* 47, no. 2 (2015): 16–23; quotation on 20. Prior to this, Jozkowski notes alarming problems with the focus on verbal consent because of traditional gender expectations in scripts to do with sexual situations: "Some men think about consent primarily in terms of how they can obtain sex instead of as a probe for their partner's agreement to or interest in sexual behavior," she writes. "Second, some of these men seemed to realize that their partners might not willingly consent to sexual activity, so they avoid a refusal by not asking. Finally, if women are waiting to be asked for their consent, as suggested by the traditional sexual script, there is a potential for non-consensual sex to occur if men are 'taking without asking' " (19).

See also Jozkowski's and her coauthors' thoughts on this same issue in the following article: Kristen N. Jozkowski, Zoë D. Peterson, Stephanie A. Sanders, Barbara Dennis, and Michael Reece, "Gender Differences in Heterosexual College Students' Conceptualizations and Indicators of Sexual Consent: Implications for Contemporary Sexual Assault Prevention Education," Journal of Sex Research 51 (2014): 904–16. Of note in this article are the authors' findings of gender differences in giving and understanding consent. "There were significant differences in how men and women indicated their own consent and nonconsent," they write, "with women reporting more verbal strategies than men and men reporting more nonverbal strategies than women, and in how they interpreted their partner's consent and nonconsent, with men relying more on nonverbal indicators of consent than women" (904). The article also discusses "traditional sexual scripts," with the authors claiming that "the dynamics of the traditional sexual script create a situation in which men are expected to ask women for their consent, women are expected to refuse sex, at least initially, and men are expected to ignore such refusals and continue to pursue a sexual encounter" (905). The authors draw interesting conclusions about the possibilities of consent education that focuses on verbal cues by claiming that verbal consent may be more "palatable" to women, because women are more accustomed to consent depending on them to be expressed, whereas men are more accustomed to situations where they don't have to indicate their consent because their consent is always (at least traditionally) assumed. "Contemporary sexual assault prevention and risk-reduction education encourages a verbal communication of consent," write the authors. "This type of education may be palatable to women, as they are more likely than men to indicate their consent via verbal cues. However, men may not be as receptive to the messages endorsed by contemporary education programming, as they may think that obtaining verbal consent seems unrealistic or unnecessary. If men's consent to sexual activity is assumed because men are assumed to always want and agree to sex, then there is no need for men to verbalize their own consent. As such, it may be difficult for men to understand the need to have verbal communications about consent as promoted by most sexual assault prevention education. Given the gender differences in consent communication, it may be more effective for educational programs to deconstruct gender-specific communication patterns so that students better understand the potential for underlying gender differences in sexual expectations and communication and the possible role of these gender differences in sexual miscommunication. Sexual assault prevention education that addresses gender differences in consent communication may help men and women see the value in direct, verbal communication of consent" (915).

For more, see also Kristen N. Jozkowski and Zoë D. Peterson, "College Students and Sexual Consent: Unique Insights," *Journal of Sex Research* 50 (2013): 517–23.

12. Melissa Burkett and Karine Hamilton, "Postfeminist Sexual Agency: Young Women's Negotiations of Sexual Consent," *Sexualities* 15 (2012): 815–33.

13. Jozkowski, "Yes Means Yes?", 21.

CHAPTER 3

1. For more on the University of Virginia's liquor ban, see Sandy Hausman, "After Rape Scandal, University of Virginia Reworks Relationship with Frats," December 2, 2014, https://www.npr.org/2014/12/02/367938662/after-rape-scandal-university-of-virginia-reworks-relationship-with-frats;   for more on Dartmouth's ban, see Matt Rocheleau, "Dartmouth College to Ban Hard Alcohol, Forbid Greek Life Pledging, among Slew of Policy Changes," *Boston Globe*, January 29, 2015, https://www.bostonglobe.com/metro/2015/01/29/dartmouth-college-ban-hard-alcohol-forbid-greek-life-pledging-among-slew-policy-changes/WCxS4OHSLK5hZ5Z7u5E8iN/story.html.

A brief note is in order on the *Rolling Stone* controversy over "A Rape on Campus," the nine-thousand-word sexual assault exposé published on November 19, 2014, about an anonymous student (called "Jackie" for the article) who told the story of her gang rape at a University of Virginia frat house, and UVA's ensuing concern over the school's reputation and possible scandal over "Jackie's" claims of sexual assault. The article was— tragically—later proved a hoax. I call it tragic not because of the fraternity and the officials on campus who were defamed because of it but because it gave a footing to fraternities and institutions, both of which already were famous for committing just these sorts of crimes, to play the role of victims, to claim that they were the ones harmed and maligned, and to levy accusations and arguments that women make false accusations of sexual assault—the occurrence of which is statistically low to negligible, anywhere from 2 percent on the low end to 10 percent on the high end. The real problem we face—as I've discussed thoroughly earlier in this book—is that victims tend not to make reports at all. For more on the *Rolling Stone* article "A Rape on Campus," see Richard Pérez-Peña and Ravi Somaiya, "Rolling Stone Cites Doubts on Its Story of University of Virginia Rape," *New York Times*, December 5, 2014, https://www.nytimes.com/2014/12/06/us/rolling-stone-re-examines-its-account-of-virginia-rape.html; Dana Will, "A Note to Our Readers," *Rolling Stone*, December 5, 2014, http://www.rollingstone.com/culture/news/a-note-to-our-readers-20141205; and for the most comprehensive assessment of what happened, see Sheila Coronel, Steve Coll, and Derek Kravitz, "Rolling Stone & UVA: Columbia School of Journalism's Report; An Anatomy of a Journalistic Failure," *Rolling Stone*, April 5, 2015, http://www.rollingstone.com/culture/features/a-rape-on-campus-what-went-wrong-20150405. For statistics on false reporting, see National Sexual Violence Resource Center, "Statistics about Sexual Violence," 2017, https://www.nsvrc.org/sites/default/files/publications_nsvrc_factsheet_media-packet_statistics-about-sexual-violence_0.pdf.

2. For criticism of and debate about these alcohol bans, see the following articles: Katie Reilly, "Why Banning Hard Alcohol on College Campuses May Not Be the Answer," *Time*, August 24, 2016, http://time.com/4463227/stanford-hard-liquor-ban/; and Jake New, "Stanford's Ban on Large Containers of Hard Alcohol Sparks Debate about Sexual Assault," *Inside Higher Ed*, August 24, 2016, https://www.insidehighered.com/news/2016/08/24/stanfords-ban-large-containers-hard-alcohol-sparks-debate-about-sexual-assault. A group of five *New York Times* reporters also did a major overview of this issue by visiting five different universities and speaking to students there in their article "No Kegs, No Liquor: College Crackdown Targets Drinking and Sexual Assault," *New York Times*, October 29, 2016, https://www.nytimes.com/2016/10/30/us/college-crackdown-drinking-sexual-assault.html.

3. Online dialogue about the relationship between drinking and sexual assault has been contentious, to say the least. One major controversy was sparked by a lengthy article by Emily Yoffe, published in 2013, about the relationship between sexual assault and binge drinking on college campuses, and how it is imperative to get around the fear of victim blaming to educate women about the reality that binge drinking and sexual assault are highly correlated. Yoffe claimed that it is irresponsible for us not to speak to college women about this connection, and that if we fail to do so, we are putting women at risk. Both Yoffe and the scholars she interviewed were careful to state that cautioning young adults about the relationship between binge drinking and the risk of sexual assault is not the same thing as "saying a woman is responsible for being sexually victimized," as one of the scholar interviewees put it. Yoffe was not claiming that women should not drink at all. In response to this article, Yoffe was called a "rape apologist," a "rape culture denialist," and a "victim blamer" (among many other things) by bloggers, one of whom, Amanda Hesse, argued that Yoffe's warnings about drinking equated to telling women never to drink, and that if they did drink, they'd get raped. See Emily Yoffe, "College Women: Stop Getting Drunk; It's Closely Associated with Sexual Assault. And Yet We're Reluctant to Tell Women to Stop Doing It," *Slate*, October 15, 2013, http://www.slate.com/articles/double_x/doublex/2013/10/sexual_assault_and_drinking_teach_women_the_connection.html; Erin Gloria Ryan, "How to Write about Rape Prevention without Sounding Like an Asshole," *Jezebel*, October 16, 2013, https://jezebel.com/how-to-write-about-rape-prevention-without-sounding-lik-1446529386; and Amanda Hesse, "To Prevent Rape on College Campuses, Focus on the Rapists, Not the Victims," *Slate*, October 16, 2013, http://www.slate.com/blogs/xx_factor/2013/10/16/it_s_the_rapists_not_the_drinking_to_prevent_sexual_assault_on_college_campuses.html. Yoffe's article and the online debate it sparked led to other writers chiming in to defend the need to discuss with women the relationship between binge drinking and sexual assault. See, for example, Emily Matchar, "Alcohol Education Is Not Rape Apology," *Atlantic*, October 17, 2013, https://www.theatlantic.

com/health/archive/2013/10/alcohol-education-is-not-rape-apology/ 280661/. For Yoffe's defense of herself, see Emily Yoffe, "Emily Yoffe Responds to Her Critics," *Slate*, October 18, 2013, http://www.slate.com/ blogs/xx_factor/2013/10/18/rape_culture_and_binge_drinking_emily_ yoffe_responds_to_her_critics.html.

4. See Freitas, *Sex and the Soul*, 21, 56–75.
5. I write about this at length in chapter 2, "The All-Purpose Alcohol Solution" (35–53), in my book *The End of Sex*.

CHAPTER 4

1. This anecdote and its accompanying dialogue are told from memory. The conversation was not taped. I have done my best to remember it as it happened, both in content and in dialogue.
2. In addition to my work and that of Lisa Wade on this issue, many journalists and scholars have written about the pervasive dissatisfaction with hookup culture on college campuses and the ways in which college students try to negotiate the culture from both within and without, as well as the various ways that they opt in and out of it. For more on this, see the following texts in their entirety: Kathleen Bogle, *Hooking Up: Sex, Dating, and Relationships on Campus* (New York: New York University Press, 2008); Laura Sessions Stepp, *Unhooked: How Young Women Pursue Sex, Delay Love, and Lose at Both* (New York: Riverhead Books, 2007). For the ways in which college students negotiate in and out of hookup culture and around it, in particular, see Jason King's excellent book *Faith with Benefits* (New York: Oxford University Press, 2017), particularly chapter 5, "There Is No Campus Hookup Culture, There Are Four" (5–17), for its nuanced description and argument that different colleges produce different hookup *cultures*. See also chapters 3, 6, 7, and 8 of my book *The End of Sex*, especially chapter 3, "Opting In to a Culture of Casual Sex" (55–74), and chapter 6, "The Virginity Excuse and Other Modes for Opting Out of Hookup Culture (Sort of)" (117–38), as well as Lisa Wade's chapters on this issue in *American Hookup*: chapter 4, "Opting Out" (92–112), and chapter 5, "Opting In" (113–33). For an

insightful perspective on hookup culture and its disappointments from the perspective of a recent college graduate, see Leah Fessler's article "A Lot of Women Don't Enjoy Hookup Culture—So Why Do We Force Ourselves to Participate?," *Quartz*, May 17, 2016, https://qz.com/685852/hookup-culture/. The article, which went viral when it came out, is based on Fessler's thesis research about hookups at Middlebury. She describes how, because of hookup culture, she spent several college years having bad sex and wondering why it didn't make her feel good or sexually liberated even though a certain brand of feminism told her it should.

3. Kathleen Bogle includes a history of how old-fashioned dating evolved into the hookup of today in her book *Hooking Up*, 11–23.

4. Lisa Wade has recently begun to make this same argument—distinguishing hookup culture from individual hookups, as well as the claim that this distinction is essential in order to understand that it's not so much individual hookups that are causing students distress and anxiety, but being caught in the culture itself that's the problem. See Wade, *American Hookup*, 18.

5. All this is not to say that committed, long-term relationships do not exist on college campuses and within hookup culture—plenty do. And it's not as though all students follow the norms of hookup without exception; students certainly play with the scripts of hookup culture and even rewrite them—to a point, if not completely—to get closer to what they actually want from sex and from their partners. For more on this, see my book *Sex and the Soul*, 136–40. See also King, *Faith with Benefits*.

6. This anecdote and its accompanying dialogue are told from memory. The conversation was not taped. I have done my best to remember it as it happened, both in content and in dialogue.

CHAPTER 5

1. Given the current tidal wave of assault and harassment accusations in the media, older men have proved this to be the case as well within the workplace. The accusations are staggering, and they keep on coming, even as I write this. It is difficult to keep up with the latest accusation to hit the news because there are so many, and confronting this reality—while

incredibly important and a long time coming—has been stunning and depressing.

2. See Michael Kimmel, *Guyland: The Perilous World Where Boys Become Men* (New York: HarperCollins, 2008). See also Michael Kimmel, *Misframing Men: The Politics of Contemporary Masculinities* (Piscataway, NJ: Rutgers University Press, 2010); and Michael Kimmel, "Why Some College Campuses Are More 'Rape-Prone' Than Others," *Atlantic*, August 24, 2015, https://www.theatlantic.com/education/archive/2015/08/what-makes-a-campus-rape-prone/402065/.

3. Michael Kimmel is the leading scholar and sociologist on the issue of men and masculinity in general, but especially with respect to college men. He has not only researched and written extensively on "guy culture" in academic publications, and is the editor of the premier journal on masculinity studies (*Men and Masculinities*), but also has worked to engage in this discussion on a popular and practical level, working with men on campus and speaking to universities across the nation about ideas and biases around masculinity. He even established the Center for the Study of Men and Masculinities at Stony Brook University in New York, where he is on the faculty, the only center dedicated to academic research of its kind in the nation (thus far). For more on this center, see its website: http://www.stonybrook.edu/commcms/csmm/. For a comprehensive list of Kimmel's publications, both popular and scholarly, see the bibliography included on his website: http://www.michaelkimmel.com/works/.

One of the other men who has led the effort to get men of all ages on board in the fight against sexual assault and sexual violence is Jackson Katz, an educator and popular speaker on this issue, and also the cofounder of Mentors in Violence Prevention, a national organization that aims to enlist men to help in sexual assault prevention. Katz's highly popular, widely viewed November 2012 TED talk has put him at the forefront of men who are speaking out on this issue. For more on Katz, see his organization's website, http://www.mvpnational.org, and watch his TED talk: Jackson Katz, "Violence against Women—It's a Men's Issue," 2012, https://www.ted.com/talks/jackson_katz_violence_against_women_it_s_a_men_s_issue.

4. Courses on men and masculinities, discussions about "toxic masculinity," and even men and masculinity centers for college men—the male version of the college women's centers that have been around for decades—are popping up at institutions across the country, often accompanied by controversy. To read more about this trend, see the special report titled "Redefining College Manhood," *Chronicle of Higher Education*, December 8, 2017, https://www. chronicle.com/specialreport/Redefining-College-Manhood/169; and the following articles: Jessica Bennett, "A Master's Degree in . . . Masculinity?," *New York Times*, August 8, 2015, https://www.nytimes.com/2015/08/09/ fashion/masculinities-studies-stonybrook-michael-kimmel.html; Lautaro Grinspan, "Campus Men's Groups Explore What It Means to Be a Dude," *USA TODAY College*, July 18, 2016, http://college.usatoday.com/2016/ 07/18/campus-mens-groups-explore-what-it-means-to-be-a-dude/.

CHAPTER 6

1. For more on the controversy around the University of Alabama Alpha Phi 2015 recruitment video, see the following article, which includes the full video embedded within it: Kristen Rein, "U. of Alabama Sorority Criticized for Recruitment Video," *USA TODAY*, August 18, 2015, https://www. usatoday.com/story/news/nation-now/2015/08/18/university-alabama-criticized-racially-homogeneous-recruitment-video/31900097/.

2. For the entire list included in the film, see Kirby Dick, *The Hunting Ground*, Chain Camera Pictures, 2015.

3. For more on this, see the extensive investigation undertaken by the *New York Times* in Walt Bogdanich, "Errors in Inquiry on Rape Allegations against FSU'S Jameis Winston," *New York Times*, April 16, 2014, https:// www.nytimes.com/interactive/2014/04/16/sports/errors-in-inquiry-on-rape-allegations-against-fsu-jameis-winston.html?_r=0.

4. Elizabeth A. Armstrong, Laura T. Hamilton, and J. Lotus Seeley, "'Good Girls': Gender, Social Class, and Slut Discourse on Campus," *Social Psychology Quarterly* 77 (2014): 100. See also Laura T. Hamilton and Elizabeth A. Armstrong, *Paying for the Party: How College Maintains Inequality* (reissue) (Cambridge, MA: Harvard University Press, 2015).

5. Armstrong, Hamilton, and Seeley, "'Good Girls,'" 101. Armstrong oversaw this research at a large, Midwestern, public university dominated by Greek life, where high-status women were defined by beauty, popularity with frat boys, heterosexuality, and whiteness. For women at the top of the social pyramid, slut discourse was a kind of weapon they could wield against other women to protect their own status as "classy," to keep their status privileged by refusing entry to other women who didn't fit the norm, and to sexually demean and disempower other women. Armstrong describes these privileged women as performing a kind of "affluent femininity." This argument of Armstrong and her colleague Laura Hamilton—that a certain class of privileged women is able to navigate hookup culture toward the end of successful sexual experimentation, which they first explored in their coauthored article "Gendered Sexuality in Young Adulthood: Double Binds and Flawed Options"—is the basis on which Hanna Rosin justifies her claims that hookup culture is essential to women's sexual empowerment. See Rosin's chapter on this, "Hearts of Steel: Single Girls Master the Hookup," in her book *The End of Men: And the Rise of Women* (New York, Riverhead Books, 2012), 17–46. But Rosin ignored the wider argument that Armstrong and her colleagues make about how only a certain class of privileged white women is able to sexually experiment, and that these women do so only at the expense of and by devaluing and shaming other women on campus, exacerbating and exploiting class differences in the process. During her research, Armstrong also learned that even the most privileged women in the party scene were still vulnerable to, and fearful of, getting labeled a slut by equally privileged peers (less privileged women didn't have the power to apply the label to the more privileged women) and were traumatized when this happened. There was a sense among privileged women that the only and the best way to be treated as a kind of sexual equal by men on campus (which came with a kind of protected status of sexual respect) was to ensure that the "classy" label applied only to them. Once this privileged label was lost, a woman could be used, abused, and discarded with impunity by men, since "slutty" women have obviously done something to deserve their demeaning status. Slut shaming is a tool wielded to protect the sexual value and respect of certain

women on campus at the expense of others as well as to punish women who violate norms around women and sex. Yet all women, even "classy," sexually privileged women, have to walk a fine line with respect to explicit expressions of sexual desire, the initiation of sex (which is still the man's job), and their number of partners. For more on the relationship between hookups, gender, privilege, and intersectionality, see also L. Hamilton and E. A. Armstrong, "Gendered Sexuality in Young Adulthood: Double Binds and Flawed Options," *Gender and Society* 23 (2009): 589–616.

6. Armstrong, Hamilton, and Seeley, " 'Good Girls,' " 118.
7. See Freitas, *Sex and the Soul*, 115, 147, 158.
8. Ibid., 126–64.
9. During my interviews, when I pressed women to tell me why they dressed according to these themes when they were so adamantly afraid of getting labeled sluts, their responses revealed how deeply they live a double standard. As women, they needed to show their approval of accepted campus norms, which required them to be casual and laid-back about sex, but they also had to be very careful with their level of participation and number of partners, lest they get labeled sluts. When I pointed out that theme parties openly did this very thing—labeled them as whores— women explained the following logic: theme parties "empower" a woman to dress sexy and act sexually available without getting stuck with the label of slut. Women were just "hos" for the evening, and the next day they were just regular college girls again. Like magic. Though, it's also true, they explained, a girl still had to be careful with her behavior so the label didn't *really* stick past the one evening.

Many women claimed they liked theme parties because they provided the only opportunities to dress sexy and act sexually available with impunity. At this, I wondered whether women wouldn't prefer to dress however they wanted and be however sexy or unsexy they so desired all the time. In my mind, this would be a sign of true empowerment: to wear whatever clothing they felt like wearing at any given moment, without having to wait for a man's permission or a party to do so. Theme parties may seem like a socially approved opportunity to dress sexy, yet they are exactly the opposite. Allowing men (or, in certain cases, a privileged group of women) on campus to determine when, where, and how a woman can dress sexy reinforces women's disempowerment around their dress and their lack of freedom to dress sexy when they want without punishment. Women's bodies continue to be sites of exploitation and objectification that remain under the control of others. But women expressed a general feeling that thwarting these rules was impractical. If a woman challenges the norms that tell her when, where, and how she can dress sexy, she runs the risk of those ever-feared labels becoming permanent.

10. See Melanie S. Hill and Ann R. Fischer, "Examining Objectification Theory," *Counseling Psychologist* 36 (2008): 745. For more on this issue, see also Sharon Lamb and Lynn Mikel Brown, *Packaging Girlhood: Rescuing Our Daughters from Marketers' Schemes* (New York: St. Martin's Griffin, 2007).

11. Hill and Fischer, "Examining Objectification Theory," 767.

12. Barbara L. Fredrickson and Tomi-Ann Roberts, "Objectification Theory: Toward Understanding Women's Lived Experiences and Mental Health Risks," *Psychology of Women Quarterly* 21 (1997): 174. See also Kim Claudat and Cortney S. Warren, "Self-Objectification, Body Self-Consciousness during Sexual Activities, and Sexual Satisfaction in College Women," *Body Image* 11 (2014): 509–15; and Laura Vandenbosch and Steven Eggermont, "Understanding Sexual Objectification: A Comprehensive Approach toward Media Exposure and Girls' Internalization of Beauty Ideals, Self-Objectification, and Body Surveillance," *Journal of Communication* 62 (2012): 869–87.

13. For more on sexual privilege, see the following: Leslie C. Bell, *Hard to Get: Twenty-Something Women and the Paradox of Sexual Freedom* (Berkeley: University of California Press, 2013); Julie Bettie, *Women without Class: Girls, Race, and Identity* (Berkeley: University of California Press, 2003); Patricia Hill Collins, *Black Sexual Politics: African Americans, Gender, and the New Racism* (New York: Routledge, 2004); Lorena Garcia, *Respect Yourself, Protect Yourself: Latina Girls and Sexual Identity* (New York: New York University Press, 2012); Jessica Ringrose and Emma Renold, "Slut-Shaming, Girl Power and 'Sexualisation': Thinking through the Politics of the International SlutWalks with Teen Girls," *Gender and*

Education 24 (2012): 333–43; Emily White, *Fast Girls: Teenage Tribes and the Myth of the Slut* (New York: Scribner, 2002).

14. See Association of American Universities, "AAU Climate Survey on Sexual Assault and Sexual Misconduct (2015)."

15. See Jake New, "Colleges Sued by Students for Negligence Turn to 'Victim Blaming' in Defense," *Inside Higher Ed*, June 17, 2016, http:// www.insidehighered.com/news/2016/06/17/colleges-sued-students-negligence-turn-victim-blaming-defense; and Eliza Gray, "Why Don't Campus Rape Victims Go to the Police?," *Time*, June 23, 2014, http:// time.com/2905637/campus-rape-assault-prosecution/.

16. Please note that the idea that "women are caught in a devil's bargain" came from reading about Matthew Desmond's use of the concept of a "devil's bargain" with respect to the relationship between poverty and eviction in his book *Evicted: Poverty and Profit in the American City* (New York: Broadway Books, 2016), 192.

17. Marissa Payne, "Erica Kinsman, Who Accused Jameis Winston of Rape, Tells Her Story in New Documentary 'The Hunting Ground,'" *Washington Post*, February 19, 2017, http://www.washingtonpost.com/news/early-lead/wp/2015/02/19/erica-kinsman-who-accused-jameis-winston-of-rape-tells-her-story-in-new-documentary-the-hunting-ground/?utm_term=.818aa18fbd5f.

18. For more information, see "Survivor Victory: Erica Kinsman Wins Historic Settlement against Florida State," *The Hunting Ground*, January 25, 2015, http://thehuntinggroundfilm.com/2016/01/erica-kinsman-wins-historic-settlement/.

19. A young woman once sat in my office and told me she was transferring because she had hooked up with the wrong person—someone who decided to brag about the encounter to the rest of the campus—and she was being tormented by her peers for it. She would wake up in the morning, and people would have written "slut" and "whore" and drawn cartoons of women giving blow jobs on the white board on the door of her dorm room in permanent marker. She'd take down the board and put up a new one, only to have it happen again. It didn't matter that she wasn't someone who hooked up regularly, or that she'd never had sex before. Nobody cared about

these things, she explained. All that mattered was that she'd become a slut to everyone, and in her mind, there was no escaping this label, at least not at this particular college. So, she told me, it was just easier to transfer and start over. When I suggested that we go to talk to her RA and one of the deans in Student Affairs about what was happening, she shook her head. It didn't matter what they did, she felt. Calling out people's actions would only turn her into more of a pariah and exacerbate the shaming she had to endure on campus. The young woman experienced both slut shaming and a fear of victim blaming. She was being punished by both women and men for a single hookup. The threat of further punishment for trying to get help from university officials made her so fearful that it stopped her from pursuing this route. She left the school, ashamed, her voice silenced, her life altered, while everyone else around her went on as though life was normal.

20. For more information about Seeberg's case: Melinda Henneberger, "Reported Sexual Assault at Notre Dame Campus Leaves More Questions Than Answers," *National Catholic Reporter*, March 26, 2012, https://www.ncronline.org/news/accountability/reported-sexual-assault-notre-dame-campus-leaves-more-questions-answers.

21. Neesha Arter, " 'The Hunting Ground' Sheds New Light on Campus Rape Epidemic," *Daily Beast*, February 26, 2015, https://www.thedailybeast.com/the-hunting-ground-sheds-new-light-on-campus-rape-epidemic.

22. One of the most transformative examples of resistance to self-blame, slut shaming, and victim blaming that has emerged is the SlutWalk. SlutWalks originated in Toronto after a police officer advised a group of college women at York University that they "should avoid dressing like sluts in order not to be victimized." Heather Jarvis decided to organize a march to protest this and similar messages. The goal was to spread the idea that a woman's dress has nothing to do with her consent to have sex. Participants don their highest heels, their shortest skirts, their most revealing tops (and men who participate usually do the same) and march down a public street or across the campus green. There are now SlutWalks on campuses all over the world. These events raise awareness of the tragedy of victim blaming; they also empower women to transform this slur, intent on demeaning them, into an expression

of pride and defiance. Sarah Millar, "Police Officer's Remarks at York Inspire 'Slutwalk,'" *Toronto Star*, March 17, 2011, https://www.thestar.com/news/gta/2011/03/17/police_officers_remarks_at_york_inspire_slutwalk.html. See also Ringrose and Renold, "Slut-Shaming, Girl Power and 'Sexualisation,'" 333–43.

23. Jonathan Mahler, "For Many Women, Trump's 'Locker Room Talk' Brings Memories of Abuse," *New York Times*, October 10, 2016, https://www.nytimes.com/2016/10/11/us/politics/sexual-assault-survivor-reaction.html?_r=0.

24. Jessica Valenti, "What Does a Lifetime of Leers Do to Us?," *New York Times*, June 4, 2016, https://www.nytimes.com/2016/06/05/opinion/sunday/what-does-a-lifetime-of-leers-do-to-us.html?_r=0. See also Jessica Valenti, *Sex Object: A Memoir* (New York: Dey Street Books, 2016).

CHAPTER 7

1. But it's also true that there is extraordinary work being done in the realm of feminist ethics, especially feminist theological ethics. For example, Rebecca Todd Peters's recent feminist theological manifesto, which offers a liberal, left-leaning argument about abortion, is extraordinary work: see Rebecca Todd Peters, *Trust Women: A Progressive Christian Argument for Reproductive Justice* (Boston, MA: Beacon Press, 2018). In my opinion, Margaret Farley's *Just Love* is essential reading on the subjects of social justice, ethics, sex, and love: see Margaret A. Farley, *Just Love: A Framework for Christian Sexual Ethics* (New York: Continuum, 2006). Kate Ott's work on raising children to be self-aware and empowered around sex in a faith context is also wonderful: see Kate Ott, *Sex + Faith: Talking to Our Kids from Birth to Adolescence* (Louisville, KY: Westminster John Knox, 2013). For more classic texts in the realm of feminist theological ethics, there is also Lisa Sowle Cahill, one of the pioneer feminist theologians in this area: see (among other books by Cahill) Lisa Sowle Cahill, *Sex, Gender, and Christian Ethics* (New York: Cambridge University Press, 1996); and also Christine E. Gurdorf, *Body, Sex, and Pleasure* (Cleveland, OH: Pilgrim Press, 1995).

2. Martha Nussbaum, one of the great philosophers of our time, has argued passionately and extensively for the role of emotions in ethical

decision-making and intelligent thought. For Nussbaum, considering emotion is essential when we are thinking about ethics. Without emotion we fail at compassion, at empathy, at intimacy, and at friendship. When Nussbaum's arguments about the relationship between emotion and ethics are framed in light of the norms that hookup culture establishes about emotional *detachment* because both emotion and attachment are *devalued*, the gulf we face between sexual decision-making and adopting an attitude that privileges consent is obvious. Consent, the *why* of it, the reasons behind it, is buoyed by those very subjects that stand at the heart of ethics for Nussbaum. See, in particular, Martha Nussbaum, *Sex and Social Justice* (New York: Oxford University Press, 2000).

CHAPTER 8

1. As an example, see Julia Kristeva, "Stabat Mater," in *The Kristeva Reader*, ed. Toril Moi (New York: Columbia University Press, 1986) 160–86.
2. Roxane Gay has an excellent opinion piece about creating "safe spaces" on campus for discussion and the subject of trigger warnings. Please see her article: Roxane Gay, "The Secution of Safety, On Campus and Beyond," *The New York Times*, 2015, https://www.nytimes.com/2015/11/15/opinion/sunday/the-seduction-of-safety-on-campus-and-beyond.html.

CHAPTER 9

1. The *New York Times* reported that, for graduation, "Columbia officials had asked [Sulkowicz] to leave the mattress behind." And when she didn't, when Sulkowicz went onstage to receive her diploma, "President Lee C. Bollinger turned away as she crossed in front of him, failing to shake her hand, as he did with the other graduates." See Kate Taylor, "Mattress Protest at Columbia University Continues into Graduation Event," *New York Times*, May 19, 2015, https://www.nytimes.com/2015/05/20/nyregion/mattress-protest-at-columbia-university-continues-into-graduation-event.html.
2. See Bernice Sandler and Roberta Hall, "The Classroom Climate: A Chilly One for Women?," 1982, *Project on the Status and Education of Women, Association of American Colleges,* https://files.eric.ed.gov/fulltext/ED215628.pdf.

CONCLUSION

1. For more information, see the website for the Association of Title IX Administrators (ATIXA): https://atixa.org/partners/conference-sponsors/.

2. Sharon Daloz Parks, *Big Questions, Worthy Dreams: Mentoring Young Adults in Their Search for Meaning, Purpose, and Faith* (San Francisco: Jossey-Bass, 2000), 6.

3. Ibid.

4. Ibid., 16.

INDEX

ABOUT THE AUTHOR

Donna Freitas lectures at universities across the United States on her work about college students. She is the author of *Sex and the Soul: Juggling Sexuality, Spirituality, Romance, and Religion on America's College Campuses* and *The Happiness Effect: How Social Media Is Driving a Generation to Appear Perfect at Any Cost*, and has written for publications including *The Wall Street Journal* and *The New York Times*. Freitas is currently a nonresident research associate at the Center for Religion and Society at Notre Dame. She lives in New York City.